Mastering Information Technology

A Practical Guide for Beginners, Professionals & Business Leaders

Learn the Language of Modern IT and Thrive in Any Career

Gold-Standard Digital Literacy Guide for Professionals

Amjid Ali

CIO | Digital Visionary | Educator | Consultant

amjidali.com

Preface

Technology has become the heartbeat of every modern organization—regardless of size, industry, or geography. Yet, after more than 25 years in the field of Information Technology, I've seen a recurring challenge in companies across the board: a disconnect between technology professionals and the rest of the organization.

Whether it's a frontline employee trying to understand a new software system, a manager confused by IT jargon, or a business owner unsure how technology aligns with strategy—the result is often frustration, delay, and lost opportunity.

I've faced these situations countless times. I've watched brilliant ideas stall because non-technical stakeholders didn't feel confident enough to engage in tech conversations. I've witnessed promising employees held back simply because they lacked exposure to digital tools. And I've seen leaders make critical decisions without truly understanding the digital foundations of their business.

This book is my humble attempt to fix that.

"Mastering Information Technology" is not just another tech manual. It's a guide—written in plain, practical language—for anyone who wants to thrive in today's digital-first workplace. Whether you're a job seeker, entrepreneur, team leader, employee, or C-level executive, this book is for you.

My goal is to **demystify IT**, not to impress you with technical complexity but to empower you with practical understanding. From basic computing and networking to ERP systems, cybersecurity, AI, and workflow automation—every chapter is designed to give you real-world knowledge that you can apply right away.

You won't need a computer science degree to understand this book. You just need curiosity, a desire to learn, and a willingness to embrace the tools shaping our professional lives.

This is not just a book. It's your companion in becoming digitally fluent and future-ready.

Whether you're setting up your first business, managing teams, or simply aiming to become more productive at work—this book will help you **speak the language of technology**, make informed decisions, and collaborate more effectively with IT teams.

Let's bridge the gap. Let's master Information Technology—together.

—Amjid Ali

CIO | Digital Visionary | Educator | Consultant

Table of Content

PART 6
DATA LITERACY AND DATA GOVERNANCE

PART 7
CYBERSECURITY AND DIGITAL SAFETY

PART 8
VIRTUALIZATION, CLOUD COMPUTING, AND CONTAINERIZATION

PART 9
AUTOMATION, AI, AND THE FUTURE OF WORK

PART 1

UNDERSTANDING THE DIGITAL WORLD

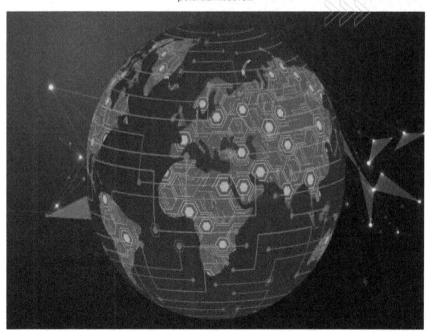

Chapter 1
What is Information Technology and Why It Matters

Information Technology (IT) refers to the use of systems, especially computers and telecommunications, for storing, retrieving, and sending information. But IT is not just about hardware and software—it is about using technology strategically to solve problems, improve productivity, and enable business growth.

In today's world, nearly every professional, regardless of their role or industry, interacts with IT in some form. Whether it's using an email platform, logging into a payroll portal, accessing customer data through a CRM system, or simply storing files on the cloud, IT underpins nearly every function in a modern workplace.

Why IT Matters

1. **Operational Efficiency**: IT streamlines processes, reduces manual work, and enhances speed. For example, a manufacturing firm using ERP software can automate inventory tracking, procurement, and production planning—all in one system.

2. **Informed Decision-Making**: Data collected through IT systems enables leaders to make smarter, faster, and more accurate decisions. For instance, a retail business can analyze sales data to identify best-selling products and optimize stock levels.

3. **Communication & Collaboration**: Tools like Microsoft Teams, Slack, and Zoom have transformed how teams collaborate, especially in hybrid and remote work models. Files can be shared in real time, meetings can be conducted across time zones, and updates are instantly accessible.

4. **Scalability & Flexibility**: Cloud-based solutions allow businesses to scale operations quickly without large capital investment. A startup can use cloud storage, virtual servers, and SaaS tools to operate like an enterprise—with a fraction of the infrastructure.

5. **Customer Experience**: From personalized marketing to 24/7 customer support chatbots, IT enhances how organizations engage and retain customers. Businesses use CRMs to track customer interactions and preferences, allowing for tailored service.

6. **Risk Management & Security**: IT systems also help manage risk—from cybersecurity frameworks to data backup solutions that ensure business continuity.

Real-World Example: A Small Retail Shop

Consider a small clothing store that installs a point-of-sale (POS) system integrated with inventory management. Every time an item is sold, inventory is automatically updated. The system generates daily sales reports, tracks customer purchase history, and even helps reorder stock based on trends. The owner, who once relied on handwritten receipts, now has access to data-driven insights, faster billing, and better control over business operations—all enabled by IT.

Real-World Example: A Multinational Corporation

In contrast, a multinational enterprise might use SAP or Oracle ERP systems to manage global operations—supply chain, finance, HR, and compliance—across countries and departments. These systems connect thousands of employees and stakeholders, delivering real-time data and automation that supports strategic decision-making at the highest level.

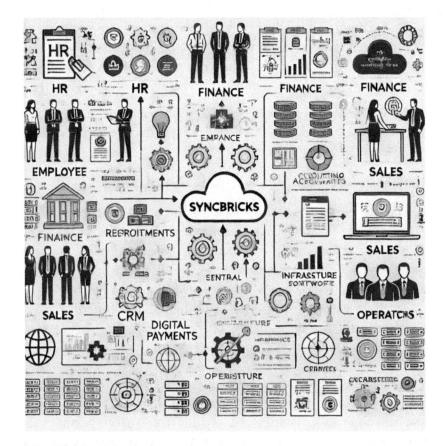

IT is No Longer Optional

In the digital age, IT is no longer a department you call when your printer stops working. It is a critical driver of business performance, innovation, and competitive advantage. This is why understanding IT—at least the basics—is no longer just a technical requirement, but a professional necessity.

In the following chapters, we will break down key IT concepts, roles, and systems so that you, regardless of your background, can confidently engage with technology in your everyday work.

Chapter 2
Common IT Terms Simplified: Hardware, Software, Cloud, and SaaS

One of the most common reasons non-technical professionals struggle with technology is that they're expected to understand technical terms without being introduced to them in a relatable way. Information Technology doesn't have to be mysterious or intimidating—it just needs to be explained in the right context.

In this chapter, we'll explore some of the most commonly used IT terms: hardware, software, cloud, and SaaS. These are foundational to every workplace today, and whether you're working in HR, sales, finance, operations, or customer service, you're already interacting with them daily.

Understanding Hardware

Hardware refers to the physical components of a computing system. If you can touch it, it's hardware. This includes the obvious things like your desktop computer or laptop, but it also extends to devices like printers, scanners, keyboards, and even networking equipment like routers and firewalls.

In a business environment, hardware forms the backbone of operations. Consider a retail store: the point-of-sale system, barcode scanner, receipt printer, and network cable connecting the system to the internet are all hardware components working together to complete a sale. When any one of them fails, the entire process is disrupted.

Similarly, in an office environment, the performance of your computer impacts your daily productivity. A slow laptop with insufficient RAM can make working with large Excel files or multiple applications feel like a chore. Many times, what appears to be a software issue is simply hardware struggling to keep up.

Professionals should also recognize the role of servers. In many companies, data and applications are hosted on physical or virtual servers located either on-premises or in a data center. These machines run 24/7, supporting everything from email systems to file sharing and ERP platforms.

What is Software?

Software is what makes hardware useful. It refers to the set of instructions or programs that tell your computer what to do. Without software, hardware is just a collection of electronic parts.

There are several categories of software that business users interact with daily. First, the operating system—such as Microsoft Windows or macOS—manages all hardware resources and provides the interface you interact with. Then there are application programs like Microsoft Word, Excel, Google Chrome, or your company's accounting system.

For example, consider a logistics company. Its dispatcher may use routing software to optimize deliveries, while the finance department uses accounting software to track payments. Meanwhile, HR may use a separate HRMS platform to manage employee data. All these are examples of application software serving specific business functions.

There are also utility programs like antivirus software, backup tools, and file recovery systems. These work behind the scenes to maintain system health and protect data.

When using any system in your workplace—whether it's a browser, a document editor, or a full-blown enterprise application—you're interacting with software. Understanding this distinction helps you troubleshoot better and communicate more clearly with your IT team.

The Shift to the Cloud

Cloud computing is one of the most transformative changes in IT over the past two decades. Instead of hosting data and applications on local servers or individual machines, businesses now rely on cloud service providers to deliver these services over the internet.

The cloud essentially means someone else's computer, accessed remotely. But it's far more than that. It offers scalability, flexibility, cost savings, and global accessibility.

Imagine a medium-sized architectural firm. Ten years ago, it might have had its own server in the office running file storage, email, and project management software. Today, the same firm likely uses Microsoft 365 for documents, Google Drive for file storage, and perhaps Autodesk's cloud-based design tools. These services are always available, always updated, and accessible from any location.

Cloud services come in various forms. Some provide storage, like Dropbox or Google Drive. Others offer processing power, like Amazon Web Services (AWS) or Microsoft Azure, which host applications, databases, and entire IT environments.

The key takeaway is this: when you use the cloud, you're renting computing resources instead of buying and managing them. It changes how organizations invest in technology and how users access it.

What is SaaS and Why It Matters

SaaS stands for Software as a Service. It's a category of cloud computing where users access software over the internet, typically through a web browser, without installing or managing the application themselves.

SaaS is the model behind most of the tools modern professionals rely on today. If you've used Gmail, Zoom, Salesforce, QuickBooks Online, or Slack, you've used SaaS.

Let's consider an HR team managing leave requests, payroll, and employee evaluations. In the past, they might have used a desktop-based HR software installed on a single machine. With SaaS platforms like Zoho People or BambooHR, they can now manage all these functions through a web interface—no installation, no upgrades, and no hardware headaches. Employees can access their profiles, submit leave requests, and download payslips from anywhere.

The benefits of SaaS are immense. The software is updated regularly by the provider. It's accessible across devices. It supports collaboration. And most importantly, it allows smaller companies to access powerful enterprise tools without heavy infrastructure investment.

However, SaaS also requires an awareness of data privacy and subscription management. Users must know how to secure accounts with strong passwords and two-factor authentication. Organizations must understand how to evaluate the reliability of a SaaS vendor, especially when sensitive data is involved.

7

Bringing It All Together

Every professional—regardless of role or seniority—uses hardware, software, cloud platforms, and SaaS products every day. A finance manager generating reports in ERP, a salesperson logging leads in CRM, a project manager reviewing tasks in Project Management software—all of them are working within this ecosystem.

Understanding these concepts helps not just in working efficiently but also in making informed decisions, requesting the right support from IT, and contributing meaningfully to technology-driven discussions.

In the next chapter, we will go deeper into how IT is structured within organizations—who does what, how systems are maintained, and how businesses keep everything running smoothly behind the scenes.

Chapter 3
How IT Works in Business: Roles, Systems, and Departments

In most organizations, Information Technology operates behind the scenes, yet it enables almost every aspect of modern business. Understanding how IT functions within a company helps professionals communicate better with technical teams, set realistic expectations, and play a more active role in digital transformation efforts.

This chapter will explain how IT is structured in a business, the various roles within an IT department, and how different systems are supported and maintained to keep operations running.

Every business, whether a small startup or a global enterprise, depends on IT to function efficiently. The scope and complexity of the IT function may vary depending on the size of the organization, but the foundational structure and responsibilities are surprisingly consistent.

At its core, the IT department is responsible for ensuring that technology works, data is safe, and systems support the organization's goals.

Let's begin by understanding some of the common roles within an IT team.

IT Support or Help Desk is the first point of contact for employees facing technical issues. Whether your printer isn't working, your email isn't syncing, or you can't access your system, it's the IT support team that steps in. They handle tickets, guide users through basic troubleshooting, and escalate issues when necessary.

Network Administrators manage internal networks, ensuring employees are connected to the internet, shared drives, printers, and other resources. They monitor network traffic, manage routers and switches, and secure internal systems from external threats. Without their work, file sharing, VoIP calls, and internet access would be unreliable or insecure.

System Administrators, often called sysadmins, are responsible for managing the organization's servers and core systems. They set up user accounts, install and update software on servers, manage system backups, and maintain critical applications. In smaller companies, this role is often combined with network administration.

Database Administrators manage the company's data storage systems. They ensure that business applications like ERP and CRM systems can access, store, and retrieve data efficiently. They also manage data backups, performance tuning, and access controls.

Software Developers or Application Developers build custom tools, automate workflows, or maintain internal platforms. Some organizations hire developers in-house, while others outsource this work to vendors. Developers may work on websites, internal dashboards, mobile apps, or integration tools that connect different systems.

Cybersecurity Professionals are responsible for protecting the company's digital assets. They monitor for threats, manage firewalls and endpoint security software, conduct risk assessments, and ensure compliance with security policies. In today's environment, where cyber threats are growing more sophisticated, this role is becoming increasingly important.

IT Managers or CIOs lead the department. They define the organization's IT strategy, manage budgets, prioritize projects, and ensure that technology is aligned with business goals. In many organizations, IT leadership is now part of the executive team, recognizing the strategic role of technology.

Beyond the IT department, companies rely on a wide range of business applications to support core functions. These applications often include enterprise resource planning (ERP) systems, customer relationship management (CRM) tools, human resource management systems (HRMS), accounting software, collaboration platforms, and communication tools.

For example, a company may use an ERP system like SAP or Oracle to manage its supply chain, finance, and HR operations. Salesforce might be used by the sales team to track leads and customer interactions. Microsoft 365 provides tools like Outlook, Teams, Word, and Excel, enabling communication and document creation across the company.

Each of these systems is supported, maintained, and often customized by the IT team. In many cases, the IT department also coordinates with software vendors, manages licenses and subscriptions, handles upgrades, and trains users.

In smaller businesses, a single IT generalist may handle all of these functions. In larger enterprises, each role may be supported by a full team.

A critical part of IT's success depends on collaboration with other departments. IT does not operate in a vacuum—it works closely with HR, finance, operations, and marketing to understand needs, develop solutions, and ensure smooth implementation. For example, when HR implements a new recruitment platform, IT is involved in setting up user accounts, configuring access controls, and integrating the system with email and calendar tools.

Real-world business continuity depends on IT being proactive, responsive, and aligned with organizational priorities. This means the IT team must not only have technical skills but also understand the business context. Similarly, non-technical professionals must gain enough IT awareness to articulate their needs and understand the tools they're using.

As organizations continue to digitize their operations, the role of IT will only grow in importance. In the next chapter, we'll discuss the common miscommunication that often arises between technical and non-technical teams—and how to bridge that gap for better collaboration and success.

Chapter 4
Bridging the Gap: Miscommunication Between IT and Business

One of the most persistent challenges in any organization is the disconnect between technical teams and business professionals. While both groups work toward the same goals, they often speak different languages, operate under different assumptions, and approach problems from vastly different perspectives. This gap can lead to misaligned expectations, project delays, underused systems, and frustration on both sides.

In this chapter, we'll explore the root causes of this miscommunication, the impact it can have, and practical ways to bridge the gap.

Miscommunication usually begins with how IT and business teams define success. For business users, success might mean having a simple tool that solves a specific problem without much effort or training. For IT, success might mean building a technically robust, scalable, and secure system that checks all the compliance boxes—even if it's slightly more complex to use.

Let's take a common scenario. A sales manager asks IT to create a reporting dashboard to track team performance. She imagines a clean visual with monthly sales figures and lead conversion rates. The IT team, meanwhile, might produce a detailed report full of filters, raw tables, and database joins—accurate, but overwhelming. The sales manager then complains it's too complicated, and the IT team feels their work isn't appreciated.

This is not an issue of competence—it's a communication gap.

One major factor is language. IT professionals are trained to use precise technical terms: APIs, latency, encryption, database normalization, uptime, bandwidth, and so on. For someone without a tech background, these words can sound like another language entirely. On the other hand, business users often use vague terms like "the system is slow" or "the file disappeared," which are frustratingly imprecise for IT trying to troubleshoot.

Assumptions also play a role. IT may assume that users understand basic system behavior, while users may assume that IT can instantly fix any problem, regardless of context. For example, if a shared file is deleted accidentally and there is no version history enabled, IT may not be able to recover it. The user, unaware of these technical constraints, may feel unsupported.

Another issue is a lack of clear requirements. Business teams sometimes request new features or systems without fully explaining their use cases, constraints, or end goals. IT teams may begin development based on partial information, only to find later that the solution doesn't meet the real need. This leads to scope creep, rework, and a loss of trust.

Organizational culture can also make the gap wider. In some workplaces, IT is seen purely as a support function, not as a strategic partner. This limits early involvement in planning and creates a reactive rather than proactive dynamic. Similarly, if IT teams isolate themselves from end users, they may miss valuable feedback and lose sight of real-world problems.

Bridging this gap requires intentional effort from both sides.

For business professionals, building basic digital literacy goes a long way. Understanding common IT terms, system limitations, and how technology projects are managed helps create realistic expectations and better conversations. Instead of saying "it doesn't work," providing specific context—like when the issue happened, what steps were taken, or what the expected outcome was—enables IT to respond faster and more effectively.

For IT professionals, learning to explain technical topics in plain language is a powerful skill. Avoiding jargon, using analogies, and demonstrating empathy builds trust. For example, explaining cloud storage as "like a shared drive you can access from anywhere" is more effective than discussing distributed file systems or virtualized storage nodes.

Successful organizations promote cross-functional collaboration. This means including IT early in business planning, involving users in testing and feedback, offering regular training sessions, and creating documentation that speaks to different audiences.

Some companies even assign "business analysts" or "product owners" to act as translators between departments. These professionals understand both business needs and technical constraints and can help design solutions that are practical and user-friendly.

Real-world success stories show that when IT and business work as true partners, the results are powerful. A well-implemented system can improve efficiency, cut costs, and enable growth. But this only happens when both sides invest in understanding each other.

The digital world requires more than just technical expertise—it demands collaboration, empathy, and shared language. In the chapters ahead, we'll continue building your IT understanding so you can bridge this gap and contribute confidently to technology-driven discussions and decisions.

PART 2

COMPUTING AND NETWORK ESSENTIALS

Chapter 5
Computing Fundamentals and Basic Troubleshooting

No matter what your role is in an organization, you interact with computers every day. From sending emails and preparing reports to accessing cloud applications and participating in video meetings, computing skills have become as fundamental as reading and writing. Yet many professionals never receive structured training on the basic concepts that keep their digital work environment running smoothly.

This chapter is designed to strengthen your foundation in computing by explaining core concepts in plain language, along with practical troubleshooting tips that can help you become more confident and independent in your daily work.

At its core, a computer is a machine that processes data and performs tasks according to the instructions given through software. It consists of hardware components like the processor (CPU), memory (RAM), storage drives (SSD or HDD), and input/output devices such as the keyboard, mouse, and screen. These components work together under the control of an operating system like Windows, macOS, or Linux.

Most workplace computers also include network connectivity (wired or wireless), which allows them to connect to printers, shared drives, cloud services, and the internet.

While modern computing has become more user-friendly, many problems still arise from simple issues that can be diagnosed and resolved without calling IT support. Let's look at a few examples.

If your computer suddenly becomes slow, the first step is to close unused applications and browser tabs. Computers have limited memory (RAM), and having too many programs open at once can cause performance issues. Restarting the device often clears temporary files and resets system processes, improving performance.

Another common issue is an unresponsive program. For instance, if Microsoft Word stops working, you can press Ctrl + Alt + Delete and open the Task Manager to force close the application. Once reopened, many programs offer autosave or recovery features to restore your work.

Connectivity issues are also frequent in offices. If you can't access a website or an internal tool, start by checking your internet connection. Are you connected to the Wi-Fi network? Is the Ethernet cable plugged in? Try opening another website or pinging a known address like google.com. If other sites work but your company's ERP is down, it could be a server-side issue rather than a problem with your machine.

Printers and peripherals also create frustration. If your document isn't printing, check if the printer is online, has paper, and is connected to your computer or network. Many times, reinstalling the printer driver or restarting both devices resolves the issue.

File management is another basic but essential area. Knowing where your files are saved—whether on your local hard drive, a network share, or cloud storage—can save time and prevent data loss. Organize your folders logically, use clear file names, and avoid saving everything to the desktop.

Backing up important data is equally vital. Even if your organization uses cloud storage, it's a good habit to keep a copy of critical files in a safe location. For personal files, external hard drives, USB drives, and services like OneDrive or Google Drive provide simple backup options.

Understanding different file formats can also reduce confusion. For example, a .docx file is a Microsoft Word document, while a .pdf is a read-only format ideal for sharing. An .xlsx file is an Excel spreadsheet, and a .pptx is a PowerPoint presentation. Knowing which format to use helps ensure the recipient can open and view your files correctly.

Another helpful area is keyboard shortcuts. Learning a few basic combinations can dramatically increase your productivity. For instance:

- Ctrl + C and Ctrl + V for copy and paste
- Ctrl + Z to undo
- Alt + Tab to switch between applications
- Ctrl + S to quickly save your work

These shortcuts not only save time but also help reduce repetitive strain by minimizing mouse usage.

Let's consider a real-world example. A project coordinator is preparing a report late at night. The Excel file crashes. Instead of panicking, she reopens Excel and finds that autosave has preserved most of her work. She restarts her laptop, closes background programs, and completes the task without needing to call IT the next morning. These basic skills not only empower her but also reduce pressure on the support team.

Being comfortable with computing fundamentals does not mean you must become an IT expert. It simply means you understand how to operate your tools effectively, how to recognize when something is wrong, and how to try simple steps before escalating an issue.

Organizations value employees who can solve problems independently, communicate clearly when they need help, and handle digital tools with confidence. The more comfortable you are with your technology, the more you can focus on your real job—whether that's managing a team, analyzing data, serving customers, or closing deals.

In the next chapter, we will move from standalone computers to connected environments. You'll learn how networks work, how the internet connects us globally, and what you should know about safe and effective network usage in a business context.

Chapter 6
Understanding Networks: LAN, Wi-Fi, Internet, and VPN

In today's workplace, almost every digital tool you use—email, file sharing, cloud applications, video calls—relies on some form of network connection. While we often take connectivity for granted, understanding how networks function can help you work more efficiently, troubleshoot basic issues, and communicate better with IT when problems arise.

This chapter explains the fundamentals of computer networks, including local networks (LAN), wireless connections (Wi-Fi), the internet, and virtual private networks (VPN). These concepts are vital to anyone working in a digitally connected environment.

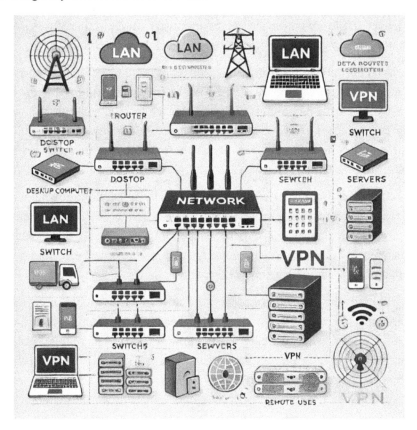

A network, in simple terms, is a system that allows computers and other devices to communicate and share data. In a business, networks connect employees to each other, to shared resources like printers and file servers, and to the wider internet.

The most common type of business network is a **Local Area Network (LAN)**. A LAN typically exists within a single building or office space and allows computers, printers, and other devices to connect through cables or wirelessly. In most offices, desktop computers are connected to the LAN via Ethernet cables, while laptops and mobile devices connect via Wi-Fi.

The router and switch are key components of the LAN. The router connects the office to the internet, while the switch helps distribute network traffic between devices inside the office. Together, they form the backbone of office connectivity.

For example, when you print a document from your laptop to the office printer, your device sends the data over the LAN to the printer. Similarly, if you open a file saved on the shared company drive, your request travels through the network to the file server and back to your computer.

Wi-Fi is the wireless form of LAN. It uses radio waves instead of cables to connect devices. In many offices, Wi-Fi enables flexibility by allowing employees to move around with laptops, tablets, or smartphones while staying connected. However, Wi-Fi can sometimes be slower or less reliable than wired connections, especially if there are many users or physical obstacles.

If you've ever experienced dropped video calls, slow downloads, or frozen web pages, the problem may be with the Wi-Fi signal. You can improve performance by moving closer to the access point, reducing interference (from walls, microwave ovens, or other electronics), or switching to a wired connection if available.

Beyond the local network is the **internet**—a global network of interconnected computers and servers. Through the internet, you access cloud services, websites, external communications, and remote systems. Your office router connects your internal network to the internet using a public IP address. From there, requests travel through service providers, data centers, and content delivery networks to reach their destination.

Here's a real-world example: You open your browser and type in your company's cloud ERP address. Your computer sends a request to your office router, which forwards it to your internet service provider (ISP). The ISP then routes the request to the cloud provider's data center, retrieves the relevant information, and sends it back through the same path to your screen. This entire process happens in seconds.

In many organizations, employees also connect to systems from outside the office—while traveling, working from home, or accessing remote offices. This is where **VPNs (Virtual Private Networks)** become important.

A VPN creates a secure, encrypted connection between your device and your company's internal network, even if you're using a public internet connection. It acts like a private tunnel through which data travels safely, protecting sensitive information from interception.

For example, a finance manager working remotely can use a VPN to securely access internal servers, process payroll, or review reports as if they were physically in the office. Without a VPN, such access would be risky and potentially expose data to unauthorized users.

VPNs are also useful when connecting over public Wi-Fi, such as at airports, hotels, or coffee shops. Public networks are often unsecured, making it easier for cybercriminals to intercept data. Using a VPN adds a layer of protection by encrypting all traffic between your device and the company network.

However, using a VPN also requires discipline. It may slightly reduce internet speed, and you should ensure that it's turned on before accessing any sensitive business systems. Many organizations provide VPN software with pre-configured settings to make this process seamless.

Understanding network basics also helps when something goes wrong. If you can't access a system, knowing whether it's a local issue (like a disconnected Ethernet cable), a Wi-Fi problem (weak signal), or an internet outage can help you provide more accurate information to IT support. It also saves time and improves response quality.

In summary, networks are the invisible highways of the digital workplace. They connect people, devices, and systems, enabling collaboration and access to critical tools. By understanding LAN, Wi-Fi, internet routing, and VPNs, professionals become more self-reliant and better equipped to work securely and efficiently in any environment.

In the next chapter, we will build on this knowledge and explore how to diagnose and resolve common network and computing issues, helping you become even more capable and confident in a digital-first workplace.

Chapter 7
Troubleshooting Network and Device Issues

Technology is at the center of modern work, but even the best systems occasionally run into problems. When something stops working—your internet connection drops, your screen freezes, or you can't print a document—it can quickly disrupt your productivity. While many issues require IT support, a large number of common problems can be diagnosed and often resolved by the user with a few simple steps.

This chapter focuses on basic troubleshooting skills that can help you handle everyday network and device issues with confidence, avoid unnecessary delays, and communicate effectively with IT when needed.

Let's begin with the most fundamental tip: **restart the device**. It may sound simple, but restarting often clears temporary errors, resets background processes, and resolves conflicts. Whether it's a slow laptop, a frozen application, or a Wi-Fi connectivity problem, restarting the device or the application in question is usually the first thing to try.

Now let's explore some typical problems and how to troubleshoot them.

1. Internet or Network Connectivity Issues

When you can't access the internet, cloud tools, or company systems, the first thing to check is your connection. Ask yourself: am I connected to the network?

If you are using Wi-Fi:

- Look at the Wi-Fi icon in the taskbar. Does it show connected, limited, or disconnected?
- If disconnected, select your office or home network and try reconnecting.
- If the signal strength is low, try moving closer to the router or access point.
- If connected but no internet, restart your Wi-Fi or router if it's a home setup.

If you are using a wired connection:

- Check if the Ethernet cable is firmly connected to both the computer and the wall or switch port.
- Try unplugging and reconnecting it.
- Look for an indicator light near the port—no light may suggest a hardware or network issue.

If others in the office are also having the same issue, it could be a wider network or ISP outage, and contacting IT is appropriate.

2. Printer or Scanner Not Working

Printer problems are frustrating but common. If your document isn't printing:

- Make sure the printer is powered on and online.

- Check if it has paper, ink or toner, and no error messages on the display panel.

- Verify the correct printer is selected in your print dialog.

- Try restarting the printer and your computer.

- If the printer is network-connected, ensure you're connected to the same network.

Similarly, scanners may not respond if drivers are missing or if the device is not detected. Reinstalling the printer/scanner drivers can often fix the problem.

3. Slow Computer Performance

A slow computer can be caused by multiple factors:

- Too many applications open: Close unnecessary programs and browser tabs.

- Low disk space: Delete old files or move them to cloud storage or external drives.

- Malware or background processes: Run a security scan or check your task manager (Ctrl + Shift + Esc) to identify heavy resource usage.

Regular maintenance like clearing browser cache, removing unused programs, and ensuring software updates are installed can keep performance stable.

4. Application Freezes or Crashes

When an application becomes unresponsive:

- Try closing it using Task Manager (Windows) or Force Quit (Mac).

- Reopen the program and check for autosaved versions of your work.

- If the issue repeats, check for software updates or reinstall the application.

In cases where a specific file causes crashes (e.g., a corrupted Excel spreadsheet), try opening it on another device or sending it to IT for recovery.

5. Audio or Video Issues During Meetings

If your microphone or camera isn't working in Zoom, Teams, or other conferencing tools:

- Check if the right microphone and camera are selected in the app settings.

- Make sure no other app is using your camera (like another open call).

- Ensure browser permissions are granted if using a web version.

- Restarting the app or the entire computer often helps reset the device configuration.

For choppy video or lagging audio, a poor internet connection is likely the cause. Switching to a wired connection or moving closer to the Wi-Fi router can improve stability.

6. Login or Access Problems

If you can't log in to a system:

- Double-check your username and password.

- Make sure Caps Lock isn't on.

- If using two-factor authentication, ensure the code is current.

- If you've recently changed your password, log out of all devices and log in fresh.

If your account is locked, expired, or permissions were removed, you'll likely need IT to intervene.

7. File Access or Sharing Issues

If you can't open a file on a shared drive:

- Confirm you're connected to the network or VPN if working remotely.

- Check whether the file is in use by someone else or marked read-only.

- Ensure you have the necessary permissions to access the folder.

Sometimes files get renamed or moved unintentionally, especially in collaborative folders. If a file has disappeared, use the search function or check the version history or recycle bin (if available).

When to Escalate to IT

While many issues can be handled independently, some require professional support:

- Hardware failure (e.g., broken keyboard, failed hard drive)

- Virus or ransomware detection

- System crashes or blue screen errors

- Application access that requires admin privileges

- Company-wide outages

In these cases, the most helpful thing you can do is provide a clear, detailed report. Instead of saying, "My system is not working," explain what you were doing, what happened, what you tried, and what the result was. Screenshots, error messages, and timestamps all help IT respond faster and more effectively.

Basic troubleshooting is not about fixing everything yourself. It's about developing awareness and confidence. The more you understand your tools, the better prepared you are to maintain productivity, reduce downtime, and work collaboratively with IT support when needed.

In the next chapter, we'll shift focus to the practical side of file organization, digital storage, and data backup—skills that can prevent problems before they happen and keep your digital workspace clean and efficient.

Chapter 8
File Management, Storage, and Backup

In the digital workplace, the way we manage our files is as important as the work itself. A poorly organized folder structure, missing document, or lost backup can quickly lead to delays, confusion, or even data loss. Yet, many professionals use computers every day without ever being taught the principles of digital file organization.

This chapter focuses on how to manage files effectively, understand the different types of storage systems, and implement simple but essential backup practices.

Every file you create or receive—be it a report, an invoice, a presentation, or an email attachment—has a digital footprint. As these files multiply over time, how and where they are stored becomes increasingly important.

Start with **file naming conventions**. Use clear, descriptive names that make documents easy to identify at a glance. Instead of saving a file as "report-final-final-revised," use names like "Sales_Report_Q1_2024" or "Employee_Onboarding_Checklist." Good file names reduce the need to open documents just to understand their contents.

Next, organize your files using a logical folder structure. Group documents by project, department, or activity. Avoid saving everything on your desktop or in a single downloads folder. For example, a marketing professional might have folders named "Campaigns," "Social Media," "Reports," and "Brand Assets." Inside "Campaigns," subfolders might be labeled by year or project name.

This hierarchy makes it easier to locate documents, collaborate with others, and reduce duplication. Consistency is key—agreeing on shared folder naming practices within a team ensures that everyone can navigate the file system confidently.

Now let's talk about **storage**. There are three primary locations where files are stored in a workplace setting:

1. **Local storage** refers to files saved directly on your computer's hard drive or SSD. While this is fast and convenient, it comes with risk. If your computer crashes or is lost, these files could be permanently lost unless backed up.

2. **Network drives** or shared folders are hosted on a central file server and are accessible to multiple users within the organization. These are commonly used in office settings where team members need to collaborate and access the same resources.

3. **Cloud storage** uses online platforms such as OneDrive, Google Drive, Dropbox, or company-specific solutions like SharePoint. Cloud storage allows for real-time collaboration, access from any device, and automatic backup features. It's particularly useful for remote or hybrid teams.

While saving files is essential, **backing them up** is what ensures their safety. A backup is simply a copy of your data stored in a separate location. If your original files are deleted, corrupted, or encrypted by ransomware, your backup is what allows you to recover.

There are several types of backup strategies:

- **Manual backup** involves periodically copying important files to an external hard drive or USB stick.

- **Cloud backup** uses services that automatically sync and store your data to the cloud.

- **Network backup** is often managed by IT, where your workstation is backed up to a server at regular intervals.

Let's take a real-world example. A finance officer stores spreadsheets related to monthly payroll on her desktop. One day, her laptop fails, and IT is unable to recover the hard drive. Because she had not backed up her files to the shared drive or cloud, weeks of work are lost. After that experience, she begins saving all key documents to OneDrive, where everything is automatically synced and backed up in real time.

Another area where awareness matters is **file formats**. Different types of files serve different purposes. Understanding which format to use helps avoid compatibility issues. For example:

- .docx is for Microsoft Word documents

- .xlsx is for Excel spreadsheets

- .pptx is for PowerPoint presentations

- .pdf is a non-editable format ideal for sharing and printing

- .jpg and .png are image files

- .zip is a compressed folder containing multiple files

When sharing documents, especially externally, converting them to PDF is often a good practice to preserve formatting and prevent unintended edits.

Many workplaces also use **version control**—keeping track of different drafts or updates of the same file. This can be manual (e.g., using file names like "Proposal_v1," "Proposal_v2"), or automated through tools like Google Docs or SharePoint, which store revision histories and allow you to revert to previous versions if needed.

Finally, always be cautious about **where** and **how** you store sensitive or confidential information. Avoid saving passwords, financial data, or private documents on unsecured personal devices or public cloud folders without proper access control. Many companies have strict data storage policies for compliance and security.

In summary, effective file management and storage habits are not only about being organized—they directly affect productivity, collaboration, and data safety. With a thoughtful approach to naming, folder structure, storage location, and backup, you can avoid many of the common frustrations and risks associated with digital work.

In the next chapter, we will explore how professionals can master the most widely used digital office tools to improve efficiency and reduce friction in daily business tasks.

PART 3

PRODUCTIVITY AND DIGITAL WORKPLACE TOOLS

Chapter 9
Mastering Word Processing: Documents, Formatting, and Templates

Word processing is one of the most fundamental skills in any professional setting. Whether you're drafting a proposal, writing meeting minutes, preparing a report, or creating an official letter, knowing how to effectively use a word processor like Microsoft Word or Google Docs can significantly enhance the clarity, professionalism, and impact of your communication.

In this chapter, we'll explore the essential features of word processing software and how to use them to create polished, consistent, and efficient documents. We'll also highlight real-world applications and common mistakes to avoid.

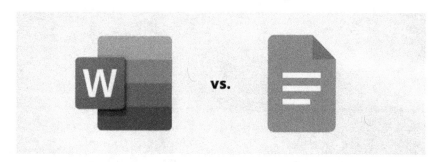

At its core, a word processor allows you to create, edit, and format text-based documents. While basic typing is easy, mastering layout, structure, and formatting features helps you move from a rough draft to a professionally presented document.

Let's begin with the basics.

Most word processing software includes familiar features: a blank page, a toolbar with fonts and styles, and tools for inserting tables, images, and page numbers. But many users only scratch the surface of what's available.

One of the most powerful yet underused features is **styles**. Styles allow you to apply consistent formatting to headings, subheadings, and body text throughout your document. Instead of manually changing font size and boldness for every section title, you can apply a predefined "Heading 1" or "Heading 2" style. This not only keeps your document uniform but also enables automatic table of contents generation.

Templates are another valuable feature. These are pre-designed layouts for common document types such as resumes, business letters, memos, and reports. Instead of starting from scratch, you can select a template and simply fill in your information. This saves time and ensures a professional appearance.

Let's consider a practical example. An HR manager preparing an employee handbook uses a standard company template that includes a title page, table of contents, and consistent formatting for section headers, body text, and disclaimers. This not only speeds up creation but makes future updates easier and ensures the document aligns with company branding.

Tables and columns help structure information clearly. Instead of listing items in a long paragraph, presenting them in a table can improve readability. For example, an operations report might include a table with columns for task names, deadlines, responsible persons, and status. Word processors allow you to insert and customize tables easily.

Images, charts, and graphics can also enhance your documents. When including visuals, always align them properly and use captions to describe their relevance. Avoid overloading your document with unnecessary decorations—clarity should always come first.

Understanding **page layout settings** is important for printed documents. Margins, orientation (portrait or landscape), and page size affect how the document appears when printed or converted to PDF. For formal documents like proposals or agreements, ensure that spacing, alignment, and page breaks are intentional and professional.

Headers and footers provide space for important information like page numbers, document titles, or your company's logo. Adding this information consistently across all pages improves presentation, especially for multi-page reports.

Word processors also offer **track changes and comments**, which are critical for collaboration. In Google Docs, these features are real-time and cloud-based, while in Microsoft Word, changes can be accepted or rejected by each participant. This is especially useful in teams where documents go through multiple revisions or require approval.

Another helpful tool is **spelling and grammar check**. While these automated suggestions are not perfect, they help catch common errors. In more advanced word processors, readability suggestions, clarity alerts, and even tone checks are available.

Let's look at a real-world scenario. A sales executive prepares a proposal for a potential client. She uses a proposal template, applies consistent heading styles, includes a cover page with the client's name and logo, and inserts tables to summarize pricing. She shares it with her manager using track changes, incorporates feedback, and finally converts the document to a secured PDF for submission. The polished, well-structured document not only reflects professionalism but increases the likelihood of winning the client's trust.

On the other hand, poorly formatted documents—mismatched fonts, inconsistent spacing, disorganized content—can damage credibility, especially in external communication.

Here are a few common mistakes to avoid:

- Manually adjusting each heading instead of using styles
- Overusing different fonts or colors
- Leaving inconsistent spacing between paragraphs
- Forgetting to insert page numbers in multi-page documents
- Ignoring spelling and grammar suggestions

For long documents, features like **bookmarks**, **table of contents**, and **navigation panes** can help you and your readers move around more easily.

In summary, mastering word processing is not just about typing quickly—it's about presenting your work with clarity, structure, and consistency. The more confident you are with document tools, the more time you save and the more professional your communication becomes.

In the next chapter, we'll turn our attention to spreadsheets, another vital tool in business environments, and explore how to use them not just for data entry but for analysis, reporting, and problem-solving.

Chapter 10
Spreadsheets Simplified: Data Entry, Formulas, Charts, and Analysis

Spreadsheets are one of the most powerful tools in the modern office. They are used for everything from budgeting and scheduling to performance tracking and data analysis. Yet many professionals only use a fraction of what tools like Microsoft Excel or Google Sheets can do.

This chapter is designed to give you a practical understanding of spreadsheets—how they work, how to use them efficiently, and how to unlock their true potential even if you're not a data expert.

At their core, spreadsheets are made up of rows and columns that create cells—each capable of holding numbers, text, dates, or formulas. What makes spreadsheets powerful is their ability to automatically calculate and organize large amounts of data using functions, formatting, and visual tools like charts.

Let's start with **data entry and formatting**. Clean data is critical. Each row should represent a single record (like a transaction or employee), and each column should represent a specific type of information (like date, amount, or department). Label your columns clearly, and avoid merging cells unnecessarily. Use consistent date formats and number formats to make sorting and filtering reliable.

Next comes **formulas**. These are the backbone of spreadsheet automation. A few simple formulas can save hours of manual calculation:

- =SUM(A1:A10) adds a list of numbers.
- =AVERAGE(B2:B20) finds the average of a set.
- =IF(C2>1000,"High","Low") provides decision-making logic.
- =VLOOKUP() or =XLOOKUP() searches for information in a table.
- =COUNTIF() counts items that meet a specific condition.

Real-world example: A sales team uses a spreadsheet to track monthly sales per employee. By entering a formula to calculate commissions based on percentages, the spreadsheet updates automatically every time new sales data is added—eliminating the need for manual recalculations.

Sorting and filtering are basic but extremely useful tools. You can sort data alphabetically or numerically, or filter it to view only what's relevant. For example, an HR manager reviewing leave records might filter the data to show only employees who have used more than 15 days of leave this year.

Conditional formatting adds color coding based on rules. You can highlight all values above a certain threshold, flag overdue items, or use color scales to show trends. A finance officer might use this to visually highlight expenses that exceed budget limits in red.

Spreadsheets also support **charts and graphs**, which help turn raw numbers into visual insights. Whether it's a pie chart for expense breakdowns or a bar chart showing monthly revenue, visuals can make reports more digestible and persuasive. Always choose the right type of chart for the story you're telling.

A **pivot table** is another powerful feature that lets you summarize and analyze large datasets. Suppose a retailer has sales data for every product, region, and month. With a pivot table, they can instantly generate a summary that shows total sales by region, by product, or by sales rep—without writing a single formula.

Data validation is useful for ensuring accurate inputs. For example, you can restrict a cell to accept only dates, or provide a dropdown list of approved department names. This reduces errors and improves consistency when multiple people are using the same file.

Another important tip is **using named ranges** and **freezing panes**. Naming ranges makes your formulas easier to understand (e.g., =SUM(Sales2024)), and freezing header rows keeps your column titles visible as you scroll through large datasets.

Collaboration is also a major advantage, especially with Google Sheets or cloud-based Excel. Multiple users can edit the same spreadsheet in real time, leave comments, and track changes. Version history allows you to restore earlier versions if mistakes are made.

Now let's consider a practical business case. A project manager creates a task tracking spreadsheet for a marketing campaign. Each row represents a task, with columns for assigned person, start date, due date, status, and notes. With conditional formatting, tasks due in the next three days are highlighted in yellow, and overdue tasks in red. Filters allow her to view only pending tasks or those assigned to a specific team member. A dashboard sheet shows total tasks completed, pending, and overdue— updated automatically using formulas. This single file becomes a live management tool, accessible to the whole team.

Despite all these capabilities, spreadsheets have their limits. As data gets larger or more complex, it may be better to use dedicated tools like databases or business intelligence platforms. But for everyday tasks, spreadsheets remain an essential, flexible tool.

Common mistakes to avoid include:

- Using inconsistent data formats (e.g., mixing text and numbers in the same column)
- Hardcoding values into formulas instead of using references
- Overcomplicating with unnecessary functions
- Failing to back up or protect important files

In summary, spreadsheets are not just for accountants or analysts— they're for everyone. Whether you're tracking performance, preparing budgets, or analyzing feedback, becoming proficient in spreadsheet tools can dramatically improve your productivity, decision-making, and communication.

In the next chapter, we'll explore how to create and deliver effective presentations—another core skill for modern professionals. You'll learn how to use tools like PowerPoint and Google Slides to communicate ideas with clarity and confidence.

Chapter 11
Presentation Tools: Creating and Delivering Impactful Visual Communication

In the modern workplace, knowing how to create and deliver an effective presentation is a vital skill. Whether you're pitching an idea, reporting on performance, training new employees, or presenting to clients, your ability to communicate clearly and persuasively using visual tools can shape how your message is received.

This chapter will guide you through the fundamentals of presentation tools like Microsoft PowerPoint, Google Slides, and similar platforms. We'll explore the essentials of structure, design, delivery, and the common pitfalls to avoid—so your presentations inform, engage, and inspire.

Let's begin with the basics. A presentation is more than a collection of slides. It is a visual aid that supports your spoken message. Your slides should enhance your communication, not replace it. A good presentation is clear, concise, visually consistent, and tailored to the audience.

Start by outlining your content before jumping into the software. Ask yourself:

- What is the purpose of this presentation?
- Who is my audience, and what do they care about?
- What action or understanding should they leave with?

Once you have your message defined, you can structure your presentation into three key sections:

1. **Introduction** – Set the context. Tell your audience what the presentation is about and why it matters.

2. **Main Body** – Break your message into clear points or sections. Use one idea per slide.

3. **Conclusion** – Summarize key takeaways, call for action, or provide next steps.

When it comes to **design**, simplicity is your best friend. Avoid cluttered slides packed with text or numbers. Use large fonts, high-contrast colors, and plenty of white space. Stick to two or three colors and one or two font styles throughout the presentation to maintain consistency.

Visual hierarchy matters. Headlines should be prominent. Supporting information should be secondary. Use bullet points sparingly—preferably not more than 3–5 per slide—and keep them brief.

Let's consider an example. A team leader is presenting a quarterly performance review. Instead of showing a spreadsheet full of numbers, she uses a line chart to highlight revenue growth, a pie chart to show cost breakdown, and a few bold statistics to emphasize key achievements. She speaks to the deeper insights while the visuals support her narrative.

Images, icons, and infographics can make your slides more engaging. Use visuals to illustrate concepts, show product features, or tell a story. However, make sure they are relevant and of high quality. Avoid clip art or low-resolution images.

Charts and graphs help simplify complex data. But choose wisely—bar charts are great for comparisons, line charts show trends over time, and pie charts display proportions. Avoid using multiple chart types on the same slide, and always label your axes, legends, and data clearly.

Another often-overlooked feature is **slide transitions and animations**. Used subtly, these can draw attention to key points. Used excessively, they become distracting. Limit animations to simple fades or appear effects and avoid spinning or bouncing elements.

Now let's talk about **delivery**. Your slides are only one part of the presentation. The other part is you—your voice, posture, tone, and engagement.

Practice your presentation in advance. Time yourself. Anticipate questions. Avoid reading from your slides—use them as prompts and speak naturally. Make eye contact (in-person or virtually), pause for emphasis, and maintain a steady pace.

If you're presenting online using Zoom or Microsoft Teams, ensure your screen is shared properly, your audio is clear, and your internet connection is stable. Close unnecessary applications to avoid notifications or performance issues during your presentation.

Speaker notes can be used to jot down key messages you want to cover for each slide. These notes are visible only to you in presenter mode and help keep your delivery smooth and focused.

Templates are another helpful feature. Most tools offer a range of slide designs, color schemes, and layouts that you can customize. Use a company-branded template if available to ensure consistency in corporate settings.

Let's consider a real-world example. A product manager is introducing a new feature to internal teams. She uses a slide deck with minimal text, clear screenshots, a customer quote, and a short demo video. She explains why the feature was developed, how it works, and what problems it solves. Her confidence, clarity, and visuals help the team understand and support the release.

Here are a few common mistakes to avoid:

- Putting too much text on each slide
- Using inconsistent formatting or colors
- Reading directly from the slides
- Overusing transitions or animations
- Including data or jargon without context

A strong presentation leaves a lasting impression. It informs, influences, and often drives decisions. Mastering tools like PowerPoint or Google Slides gives you the ability to structure your ideas visually and communicate them effectively.

In summary, great presentations are a combination of preparation, thoughtful content, clean design, and confident delivery. As you build these skills, you'll find that your ability to lead, persuade, and educate others improves significantly.

In the next chapter, we'll explore how to manage email and calendars effectively—a critical part of digital productivity that's often overlooked but can have a big impact on your daily efficiency.

Chapter 12
Email and Calendar Management: Staying Organized and Professional

Email remains one of the most essential tools in business communication, despite the rise of messaging apps and collaborative platforms. Likewise, calendar management is critical for planning, coordination, and time management. Yet many professionals struggle with overflowing inboxes, missed appointments, or unclear communication.

This chapter will help you use email and calendar tools more effectively. You'll learn practical tips for managing your inbox, writing professional messages, scheduling and organizing meetings, and using tools like Microsoft Outlook, Gmail, and calendar apps to stay on top of your tasks and relationships.

Let's start with **email**.

Your email inbox is more than just a communication tool—it's often a record of work decisions, client interactions, approvals, and deliverables. But without structure, it can become a source of stress.

Begin by organizing your inbox. Create folders or labels to group messages by project, client, department, or urgency. Archive old messages and use filters to automatically sort incoming emails. For example, emails from HR can be labeled and routed to an HR folder, while system notifications can skip the inbox entirely.

Unsubscribe from newsletters or promotional emails you no longer read. Set up rules to flag or color-code important senders—such as your manager, key clients, or vendors—so you don't miss their messages.

When it comes to writing emails, **clarity and tone** matter. Always include a meaningful subject line that reflects the content, such as "Updated Budget Proposal – Q3 2024" or "Meeting Request: Sales Strategy Review." This helps recipients prioritize and locate emails quickly.

Structure your message professionally:

- Begin with a greeting ("Dear Sarah," or "Hi James,")

- State the purpose of your email clearly in the first line

- Use bullet points or short paragraphs for readability

- Be polite but direct

- End with a clear closing or call to action ("Please confirm by Friday," "Let me know if you need further details," etc.)

Always proofread before hitting send. Typos, missing attachments, or unclear language can damage your credibility. Use the "Undo Send" feature if available—it can be a lifesaver.

Be mindful of **email tone**. Without voice or body language, written communication can be misinterpreted. Adding a polite opening and closing, and using neutral, respectful language, helps maintain professionalism.

When replying to emails, consider whether "Reply All" is necessary. Avoid cluttering inboxes unnecessarily. Use CC and BCC carefully—CC when someone needs visibility, and BCC when you want to hide recipients (such as for bulk communications).

Also, be cautious with **confidential information**. Don't forward sensitive data without authorization, and avoid clicking on unknown links or attachments—this is a common method for phishing attacks.

Now let's move to **calendar management**.

Your calendar reflects your priorities. Keeping it up to date helps you manage your time, avoid conflicts, and stay prepared for meetings and deadlines.

Use your digital calendar—Outlook, Google Calendar, or others—to schedule all work-related activities, not just meetings. Block time for focused work, project deadlines, report writing, or training. This prevents others from scheduling over your critical tasks and helps you plan your day effectively.

When scheduling a meeting, always:

- Include a clear subject and agenda in the invite

- Set the right time zone if working across regions

- Add video conferencing links if it's a remote meeting

- Attach any reference documents in advance

If you receive an invitation, respond with "Accept," "Decline," or "Tentative." Leaving it unanswered creates confusion for the organizer.

For recurring meetings, such as weekly check-ins, monthly reviews, or project updates, set up repeating calendar events. This reduces scheduling overhead and ensures consistency.

Use **reminders and alerts** to prepare in advance. Most calendar tools allow you to set notifications minutes or hours before the meeting.

A real-world example: A project manager has a packed week with client calls, team meetings, and reporting tasks. She blocks two hours each morning as "Focus Time" to work on deliverables without interruption. She color-codes her meetings by type (client, internal, personal) and shares her calendar with her assistant, so they can coordinate scheduling without back-and-forth emails. As a result, her week runs smoothly, and she feels more in control of her time.

For team-wide transparency, shared calendars are invaluable. You can see colleague availability, book conference rooms, or coordinate time off without manual tracking.

A few final tips for managing email and calendars:

- Don't use your inbox as a to-do list—separate task tracking is more effective

- Use email signatures with your name, title, and contact details

- Review your calendar at the start and end of each day

- Set clear work hours and don't feel pressured to reply instantly outside of them

- Protect your private calendar events by marking them as "Private"

In summary, mastering email and calendar tools allows you to communicate better, stay organized, and manage your time more effectively. These skills signal professionalism and reliability—qualities that make a difference in every workplace.

In the next chapter, we'll explore collaboration platforms like Microsoft Teams, Slack, and Zoom—tools that are shaping the future of teamwork in both office and remote environments.

Chapter 13
Collaboration Tools: Working Together in a Digital World

The modern workplace relies heavily on digital collaboration tools. Whether your team is in the same office or spread across cities or countries, tools like Microsoft Teams, Slack, Zoom, Google Workspace, and others have become essential for communicating, sharing ideas, and completing work together.

In this chapter, we'll explore how these tools support real-time collaboration, the differences between various platforms, and how to use them effectively in your daily work. Understanding these tools isn't just about mastering technology—it's about improving how you work with others.

Let's begin with **why collaboration tools matter**.

In traditional work environments, collaboration happened in hallways, meeting rooms, or over phone calls. Today, it happens on shared documents, in group chats, during video calls, or through task boards. These tools allow teams to:

- Communicate instantly
- Share documents securely
- Assign and track tasks
- Host virtual meetings and webinars
- Centralize conversations and decisions

Let's look at a few of the most common tools.

Microsoft Teams is widely used in businesses that rely on Microsoft 365. It combines chat, video conferencing, file sharing, and integration with Word, Excel, SharePoint, and other Microsoft apps. You can create "Teams" based on departments or projects, and within each team, you can have "Channels" for different discussions. Files shared in a channel are stored in an organized way and are available to all team members.

Slack is another popular collaboration tool, especially in tech companies and startups. It organizes communication into "channels" and allows integrations with hundreds of third-party tools like Google Drive, Trello, GitHub, and more. Conversations in Slack feel more casual, making it great for quick questions and updates, but it also supports structured work with reminders, pinned messages, and bots.

Zoom, **Microsoft Teams**, and **Google Meet** are leading tools for video conferencing. They support virtual meetings, screen sharing, breakout rooms, and recording features. Video calls are now part of daily business life—for interviews, presentations, training, and even informal check-ins.

Let's consider a real-world scenario. A marketing team is preparing a campaign launch. They create a shared folder on Google Drive for content drafts, use Slack for daily updates, meet twice a week on Zoom to review progress, and track tasks using Trello. Everyone knows what they're responsible for, and they can access everything from anywhere. Collaboration happens in real time, without email chains or delays.

Here are some **best practices** for using collaboration tools effectively:

1. **Use the right tool for the task.**
   - Use chat for quick updates or informal questions.
   - Use video calls for complex discussions or decision-making.
   - Use shared documents or boards for planning and tracking progress.

2. **Be organized.**
   - Keep channels or teams focused on specific topics or projects.
   - Use clear naming conventions for files and folders.
   - Pin important messages or announcements.

3. **Respect boundaries.**
   - Avoid sending non-urgent messages outside of work hours.
   - Use status indicators (like "Do Not Disturb" or "Away") to signal availability.
   - Don't expect instant replies unless it's time-sensitive.

4. **Be clear and concise.**

- Use bullet points or short paragraphs when sending updates.

- Tag people directly using @mentions to get their attention.

- Avoid sending too many messages one after another—bundle your thoughts.

5. **Document and share outcomes.**

- After meetings or key discussions, summarize the decisions and next steps in the appropriate channel or document.

- This helps everyone stay aligned, especially those who may have missed the meeting.

6. **Use shared calendars and scheduling tools.**

- Book meetings based on people's availability.

- Use scheduling links when needed.

- Record meetings (with consent) for future reference, especially if team members are in different time zones.

One challenge of digital collaboration is **over-communication**. Too many channels, messages, or notifications can overwhelm people. That's why teams should agree on norms—where to post what, when to use email versus chat, and how quickly to respond.

Security and access control are also critical. Only invite necessary people to shared folders or meetings. Remove access for former employees. Keep confidential files restricted and encrypted when needed.

Collaboration tools are not just for knowledge workers. Field staff, remote employees, and freelancers also benefit when communication is centralized and accessible. With mobile apps, these tools extend beyond the office and empower productivity on the go.

In summary, mastering digital collaboration tools helps you become a more effective teammate, manager, or contributor. It reduces friction, shortens feedback loops, and creates a transparent, inclusive work environment.

In the next chapter, we'll shift our focus from tools to behavior—with a look at digital communication etiquette and how to maintain professionalism and clarity in all your digital interactions.

Chapter 14
Digital Communication Etiquette: Clarity, Tone, and Professionalism in the Modern Workplace

As more workplace interactions move online, the way we communicate has changed. Emails, chats, comments, video calls, and collaborative documents have replaced many face-to-face conversations. But while the medium has changed, the need for professionalism, clarity, and respect has not.

This chapter explores digital communication etiquette—how to write and respond in a way that is effective, respectful, and appropriate for different platforms. Poor digital behavior can lead to misunderstandings, delays, and even conflict. Good etiquette, on the other hand, builds trust, improves collaboration, and enhances your professional image.

Let's begin with the foundation of all workplace communication: **tone**.

Tone is how your message feels to the reader. In person, tone is conveyed by facial expressions, body language, and voice. In digital messages, your words carry all the weight. That's why it's important to be intentional about how you phrase your messages—especially when giving feedback, making requests, or discussing problems.

Here's a simple example:

- "I need this now." (may sound demanding)

- "Can you please send this over by the end of the day?" (more respectful)

- "Would it be possible to get this today? Let me know if that's tight." (shows empathy)

In fast-moving chats or emails, it's easy to sound abrupt. But taking a few extra seconds to add a greeting, use polite language, and thank the recipient makes a big difference.

Greeting and closing matter, especially in formal communication. A simple "Hi Sam," or "Good morning," sets a professional tone. Closing with "Best regards," "Thank you," or "Looking forward to your response" adds warmth and clarity.

Be concise, but not cold. Long, rambling messages are hard to follow. But overly short replies—like "Okay" or "Noted"—can come across as dismissive. Try to balance brevity with context.

Let's look at digital etiquette across different tools.

Email:

- Use a clear subject line that matches the message content.

- Don't "Reply All" unless necessary.

- Avoid writing in all caps—it feels like shouting.

- Don't forward sensitive information without permission.

- Double-check recipients before sending.

- Use "CC" and "BCC" properly—don't expose email addresses unnecessarily.

Chat or Instant Messaging (e.g., Teams, Slack):

- Keep messages focused and professional, even if informal in tone.
- Use emojis sparingly—only when appropriate for your company culture.
- Avoid sending multiple one-line messages rapidly. Group your thoughts.
- Don't expect instant replies; everyone has different workloads.
- Respect "Do Not Disturb" and availability indicators.

Video Conferencing:

- Be on time. Join a few minutes early to test audio and video.
- Mute yourself when not speaking.
- Use your camera when possible—it creates connection.
- Dress appropriately, even when remote.
- Be aware of your background and surroundings.
- Avoid multitasking during meetings—others can usually tell.

Collaborative Documents and Comments:

- Be constructive when suggesting changes. Instead of "This is wrong," say "Consider rephrasing this for clarity."
- Use comments for feedback, not criticism.
- Track changes or suggestions if the platform allows it.
- Don't overwrite someone's work without discussion.
- Give credit when others contribute meaningfully.

Another important area is **tone awareness in cross-cultural or multi-generational teams**. What sounds neutral or humorous in one culture may be interpreted differently in another. Emojis, exclamation points, and slang should be used carefully, especially in formal communication or with people you don't know well.

Response time is another subtle but important element. You don't need to respond instantly, but do try to acknowledge important emails or messages within a reasonable timeframe—even if it's just to say, "I'll get back to you shortly."

Let's consider a real-world example. A project lead writes an urgent message to a colleague at 10 PM asking for last-minute revisions. The colleague, feeling stressed and caught off guard, reacts defensively. The next day, tensions rise. The issue could have been avoided with a well-timed message during business hours, phrased respectfully, with a realistic deadline.

Also be aware of your **digital footprint**. Everything you write, post, comment, or share in professional platforms reflects on you and your organization. This includes messages in shared chats, updates in project management tools, and content on social platforms like LinkedIn.

Here are a few final tips:

- If something can lead to confusion, pick up the phone or request a video call.
- Don't assume tone—ask for clarification before reacting.
- When emotions are high, wait before replying. Re-read your message first.
- Always recheck for typos, broken links, or missing attachments.
- Know when to escalate—and when not to.

In summary, digital communication etiquette is about being thoughtful, clear, and respectful across all platforms. It's not about being overly formal—it's about being human, even when you're working behind a screen. When done right, it strengthens relationships, builds credibility, and helps teams collaborate more effectively.

In the next chapter, we'll explore how to interpret and use data in the workplace—an increasingly important skill as organizations become more data-driven in their decision-making.

PART 4

ERP AND BUSINESS APPLICATIONS

Chapter 15
Introduction to ERP Systems: The Digital Backbone of Modern Business

Enterprise Resource Planning (ERP) systems are the heart of modern businesses. They unify data, streamline processes, and connect departments through a centralized platform. While the term may sound complex, at its core, an ERP system simply brings everything together—finance, sales, inventory, HR, procurement, and more—so that everyone works with the same data and follows consistent processes.

Whether you're in accounting, operations, sales, or management, understanding how ERP systems work is essential for working effectively in a digitally connected organization.

What is an ERP System?

An ERP (Enterprise Resource Planning) system is a suite of integrated applications that help businesses manage core functions in real-time. It acts as a central hub for storing and accessing organizational data, replacing fragmented tools like spreadsheets or standalone systems.

Instead of using separate software for accounting, inventory, payroll, and customer management, ERP systems provide a single solution to manage all of them with shared data and workflow consistency.

Key Characteristics of ERP Systems

- **Integrated Modules**: Each function (like finance, sales, or HR) is handled in a module that shares data across the system.

- **Real-Time Information**: Data updates across modules instantly, reducing delays and manual entries.

- **Standardized Workflows**: ERP enforces business processes based on predefined rules and approvals.

- **Auditability and Traceability**: Every action and transaction is logged, supporting transparency and compliance.

Common ERP Modules

1. **Finance and Accounting** – Manage ledgers, payables, receivables, bank reconciliation, and financial reporting.

2. **Sales and CRM** – Handle quotes, sales orders, invoices, and customer relationship management.

3. **Purchasing** – Manage vendor relationships, purchase orders, and procurement.

4. **Inventory and Warehouse** – Monitor stock levels, warehouse operations, transfers, and batch tracking.

5. **Human Resources** – Track employee records, attendance, payroll, and leave management.

6. **Projects and Services** – Plan, track, and bill project-based work or field service tasks.

7. **Manufacturing** – Manage bills of materials (BOM), production planning, and shop floor control.

8. **Reporting and Dashboards** – Visualize KPIs, performance data, and real-time operational insights.

Why Organizations Use ERP

ERP systems solve many common business challenges:

- Duplicate data entry across departments
- Inconsistent reports due to fragmented tools
- Lack of visibility into operations
- Delays in decision-making due to disconnected systems
- Inefficiencies from manual, error-prone workflows

By consolidating processes, ERP helps businesses become more agile, accurate, and data-driven.

Examples of ERP Systems

Some of the widely used ERP platforms include:

- SAP

59

- Oracle NetSuite

- Microsoft Dynamics 365

- Odoo

- ERPNext

- Zoho ERP

- Sage

- Infor

There are also industry-specific ERP systems tailored for retail, healthcare, construction, education, and manufacturing sectors.

ERP in Action – A Simple Use Case

Consider a retail business that uses an ERP system:

1. A **customer** places an order via the sales module.

2. The **inventory module** checks available stock and reserves the items.

3. The **finance module** creates an invoice and tracks payment status.

4. The **warehouse module** schedules a delivery.

5. The **CRM module** logs the customer's order history for future marketing.

6. A **dashboard** updates the sales manager on order performance.

This seamless flow happens without the need to switch systems or duplicate data.

Challenges and Considerations

While ERP brings immense benefits, it also requires:

- Clear understanding of business processes

- Organizational change and training

- Proper implementation and configuration

- Ongoing maintenance and support

ERP systems are not one-size-fits-all. A rushed or poorly planned implementation can lead to high costs and resistance from users.

Who Should Understand ERP?

ERP knowledge isn't just for IT or finance departments. Everyone from sales staff to warehouse teams, HR officers, and senior leadership must understand how their actions fit into the broader ERP workflow. It helps:

- Reduce errors and avoid duplication
- Improve interdepartmental coordination
- Speed up approvals and decisions
- Make better use of data in your daily role

In Summary

ERP systems are foundational tools for modern business operations. They bring structure, consistency, and visibility to organizational processes, allowing teams to work in harmony using shared data and workflows. In the following chapters, we'll explore each key ERP module in more detail, starting with the sales process and how businesses manage customer orders through an ERP system.

Chapter 16
Sales Order Processing: From Customer Request to Delivery and Billing

Sales are the lifeblood of every business, and efficient sales order processing is essential to ensure customer satisfaction, timely revenue recognition, and operational accuracy. In ERP systems, the sales process is not just about issuing invoices—it's a coordinated workflow that touches inventory, finance, logistics, and customer service.

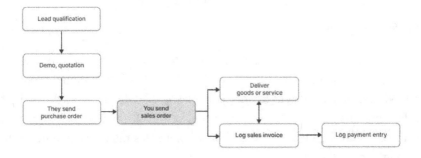

This chapter explores how sales orders are created, processed, fulfilled, and tracked within an ERP system, and how the entire sales workflow becomes streamlined when properly managed.

What is Sales Order Processing?

Sales order processing refers to the set of steps a business follows to capture a customer order, confirm it, deliver the product or service, and issue an invoice. This end-to-end workflow is typically managed within the ERP's **Sales** or **Sales and Distribution** module.

A standard sales cycle in an ERP includes:

1. **Quotation** (optional)
2. **Sales Order Creation**
3. **Inventory Check and Reservation**
4. **Delivery Note / Dispatch**

5. **Sales Invoice Generation**

6. **Payment Recording**

Step-by-Step Workflow

1. **Quotation or Estimate (Optional)**

   Before confirming a sale, businesses may issue a quote with product pricing, terms, and delivery estimates. ERP systems allow storing quotations, which can later be converted into sales orders if approved by the customer.

2. **Sales Order Creation**

   The sales team creates a sales order document in the ERP. This includes:

   o Customer details

   o Product or service items

   o Quantity and pricing

   o Delivery schedule

   o Terms and conditions (taxes, discounts, payment method)

   o The system checks for any credit limits, duplicate orders, or special pricing.

3. **Inventory Check and Allocation**

   The ERP verifies if the requested items are in stock. If available, it reserves (allocates) them for this order. If not, the order may be marked as **backordered** or **pending procurement**.

4. **Delivery Note or Dispatch Document**

   A delivery note is generated to authorize warehouse staff to pack and dispatch goods. This step may trigger barcode scanning, logistics arrangements, and vehicle scheduling. In service businesses, this step may represent assignment of a team or technician.

5. Sales Invoice Generation

6. After delivery, the system allows the creation of a **sales invoice**, which becomes the formal demand for payment. Some systems support:

   o   Partial invoicing (for phased deliveries)

   o   Combined invoicing (multiple deliveries to a customer)

   o   Automatic accounting entries in the finance module

7. Payment Entry and Reconciliation

Once the customer pays (via bank, online, or cash), the **Accounts Receivable** module is updated, and the payment is linked to the invoice. ERP systems support aging reports, dunning (reminder) processes, and overdue tracking.

Real-World Example

A furniture supplier receives an online request from a corporate client. The sales team prepares a quote. After approval, a sales order is created for 20 office chairs and 10 desks. The ERP reserves stock, generates a delivery note, and coordinates with the warehouse team. After dispatch, an invoice is sent to the client. The finance team monitors payment and sends a reminder after 14 days. The client pays via bank transfer, and the payment is recorded against the invoice.

All departments involved—sales, warehouse, finance—use the same ERP platform to manage their part of the process without duplication.

Key Features in ERP Sales Modules

- **Customer Master Data**: Stores contact info, tax details, credit limits, and order history

- **Pricing Rules**: Define discounts, special rates, tax rules, and promotional offers

- **Approval Workflows**: Require manager approval for high-value or high-risk orders

- **Shipping Integration**: Link to courier APIs or internal fleet management

- **Return Management**: Allow reverse workflows for returns and credit notes
- **Sales Analytics**: View sales trends, order conversion rates, and customer behavior

Benefits of ERP in Sales Processing

- Reduces manual errors and paperwork
- Speeds up order fulfillment
- Improves customer communication and tracking
- Supports real-time inventory visibility
- Connects sales data with financial reporting
- Enables sales forecasting and planning

Common Challenges and Solutions

- **Incorrect Data Entry**: Controlled through dropdowns, validation rules, and required fields
- **Duplicate Orders**: ERP alerts users when the same customer places similar orders
- **Stock Shortages**: Automated reorder levels or integration with procurement to trigger POs
- **Delayed Invoicing**: Auto-generation of invoices post-delivery reduces delays

Who Uses the Sales Module?

- **Sales Executives** – Create and track quotations and orders
- **Sales Managers** – Review performance, approve large deals, monitor margins
- **Warehouse Teams** – Use delivery notes to process shipments
- **Finance Teams** – Generate and reconcile invoices
- **Customer Service** – Access order status and respond to inquiries

In Summary

Sales order processing in an ERP system provides a structured, transparent, and efficient way to manage customer orders from start to finish. It ensures that every stakeholder works from the same system, with accurate data, and clear responsibilities. Whether you're in sales, support, logistics, or finance, understanding this workflow helps you serve customers better and contribute to smoother business operations.

In the next chapter, we'll explore the **purchase order process**, focusing on how businesses manage vendors, control spending, and maintain supply chain continuity through ERP systems.

Chapter 17
Purchase Order Processing: Managing Procurement Through ERP

Just as sales orders drive the revenue side of a business, purchase orders (POs) drive procurement—the process of sourcing goods and services needed to operate. Whether it's buying raw materials, office supplies, or external services, efficient procurement ensures that operations run smoothly, stock levels are maintained, and spending is controlled.

In an ERP system, the purchase module streamlines the entire procurement cycle, from requesting quotes to receiving items and recording payments. It ensures visibility, accountability, and data-driven control over what a business buys, from whom, at what cost, and under what terms.

What is a Purchase Order (PO)?

A purchase order is a formal document generated by the buyer (the business) to order goods or services from a supplier. It includes key information such as item details, quantity, price, delivery terms, and payment conditions. Once accepted by the supplier, the PO becomes a legally binding agreement.

In ERP, POs are typically created and managed through a structured procurement workflow, often including approval stages, vendor validation, and integration with inventory and accounts payable.

Typical Purchase Workflow in ERP

1. **Purchase Request / Material Request**

   The process usually begins with a need: raw materials for production, office supplies, spare parts, etc. A department raises a **purchase request** (also called a requisition) in the ERP system, specifying what they need and why.

2. **Request for Quotation (RFQ)**

   If the item is not already covered by a contract, the procurement team can send out an RFQ to multiple vendors directly from the

ERP. Vendors submit their quotes, which are compared based on price, delivery, quality, and other terms.

3. **Supplier Selection**

   The team chooses the best vendor based on system criteria or manual evaluation. Approved vendors are usually part of the **supplier master** database, which stores their certifications, history, payment terms, and ratings.

4. **Purchase Order Creation**

   Once a supplier is selected, a PO is created in the system. The PO includes:

   o   Vendor details

   o   Item description, quantity, unit price

   o   Delivery location and timeline

   o   Tax and payment terms

   o   Approval authority (if required)

   The PO is electronically sent to the vendor or printed and mailed.

5. **Goods Receipt Note (GRN) / Material Receipt**

   When the items arrive, warehouse staff logs a **Goods Receipt** in the ERP. This step ensures:

   o   Quantity and quality match the PO

   o   Inventory is updated

   o   Any shortages or damages are reported

   o   The finance team is notified for the next step

6. **Purchase Invoice and Payment**

   The supplier sends an invoice, which is matched against the PO and GRN. Once verified, the payment is processed and recorded in the ERP's **Accounts Payable** module.

Real-World Scenario

A construction company needs cement for an ongoing project. The site engineer raises a material request through the ERP. The procurement officer issues an RFQ to three suppliers. Quotes are received, and the lowest compliant vendor is chosen. A PO is generated, approved, and sent. The supplier delivers the cement, which is logged by the warehouse. After quality check, the finance team processes the invoice, and payment is made within agreed terms. All steps—from request to payment—are tracked in the ERP.

Key Features of the Purchase Module

- **Approval Workflows** – Control who can approve which purchases based on value, department, or item type

- **Vendor Rating and History** – Track delivery times, quality scores, and payment behavior

- **Budget Control** – Warn if a purchase exceeds the allocated budget

- **Contract Management** – Handle recurring purchases or pre-negotiated vendor agreements

- **Three-Way Matching** – Automatically compare PO, GRN, and invoice to prevent overpayment or fraud

- **Inventory Integration** – Update stock levels and trigger reorders

Why ERP is Critical for Procurement

Without ERP, procurement becomes reactive and error-prone. An integrated ERP system helps:

- Prevent duplicate or unauthorized purchases

- Standardize procurement across departments and locations

- Improve vendor relationships with on-time payments

- Reduce inventory holding costs

- Provide audit trails for every purchase

Common Challenges and How ERP Helps

- **Manual errors or delays** – Controlled by validation rules and automated flows

- **Lost paperwork or mismatched records** – Solved through centralized digital documents

- **Unauthorized spending** – Prevented by role-based access and approvals

- **Vendor disputes** – Avoided with documented order terms and status tracking

Who Uses the Purchase Module?

- **Department Users** – Raise requests for required items

- **Procurement Officers** – Handle vendor communication, quote evaluation, and PO issuance

- **Warehouse Teams** – Receive and inspect deliveries

- **Finance Staff** – Validate invoices and manage payments

- **Management** – Monitor spending and supplier performance

In Summary

Purchase order processing through ERP creates a clear, auditable trail from need to fulfillment. It ensures that organizations buy the right items, at the right price, from the right vendors—while maintaining transparency and cost control. Whether you're in procurement, finance, or operations, understanding how this workflow works in an ERP system helps improve planning, compliance, and efficiency.

In the next chapter, we'll explore **Customer Relationship Management (CRM)**—a critical module that helps businesses manage leads, nurture clients, and enhance customer satisfaction.

Chapter 18
Customer Relationship Management (CRM): Building and Managing Client Connections

In any organization, relationships with customers are vital. From the first inquiry to long-term engagement, managing how you interact with customers can be the difference between growth and stagnation. The **Customer Relationship Management (CRM)** module in ERP systems helps organizations attract, manage, retain, and support customers through an organized and data-driven approach.

This chapter explores the CRM functionality in ERP systems, explaining how businesses handle leads, opportunities, communication, and customer support—all while ensuring continuity, traceability, and service quality.

What is CRM in an ERP Context?

CRM refers to the tools and processes used to manage a company's interactions with current and potential customers. In an ERP, the CRM module ensures these interactions are connected to other functions like sales, support, projects, invoicing, and delivery.

Where standalone CRM systems focus purely on customer engagement, an ERP-based CRM connects that engagement with operational workflows, creating a full view of the customer journey.

Core Functions of CRM in ERP

1. Lead Management

Leads are potential customers—individuals or businesses who've shown interest in your products or services. ERP systems allow you to:

○ Capture leads from websites, emails, calls, or campaigns

○ Assign leads to salespeople

- ○ Set priorities based on region, product, or urgency
- ○ Track follow-ups and status

2. Opportunity Tracking

When a lead shows intent to purchase, it becomes an opportunity. CRM tools help manage:

- ○ Expected value of the deal
- ○ Probability of closure
- ○ Estimated closing date
- ○ Products or services involved
- ○ Competitors and challenges

Opportunities can be analyzed to forecast revenue and identify bottlenecks in the sales pipeline.

3. Customer Master and Contact Database

ERP CRM modules maintain a centralized database of:

- ○ Company details
- ○ Contact persons and decision-makers
- ○ Communication history
- ○ Industry and segmentation
- ○ Credit limits and financial behavior (linked to accounting)

4. Activity Logging and Reminders

Sales teams can log every customer interaction—emails, calls, meetings, site visits—with notes and next steps. The system can:

- ○ Send reminders for follow-ups
- ○ Track conversation history across team members
- ○ Maintain a communication trail for compliance and transparency

5. Campaigns and Email Marketing

Some ERP CRMs allow basic email marketing tools or integrate with platforms like Mailchimp. Users can:

○ Create and schedule email campaigns

○ Segment customers by location, purchase history, etc.

○ Track open rates and responses

○ Measure campaign ROI

6. Customer Support and Issue Tracking

Post-sale service matters. CRM modules in ERP can include:

○ Ticket management for complaints or queries

○ SLA (Service Level Agreement) tracking

○ Knowledge base and FAQs

○ Escalation workflows and response metrics

Real-World Example

A training company receives an inquiry through its website from a corporate HR manager. The ERP CRM captures the lead and assigns it to a sales executive. The salesperson schedules a meeting and logs it in the system. After discussions, an opportunity is created with a proposal for a 3-month leadership program.

The client agrees, and a sales order is generated. Post-program, the same CRM is used to gather feedback and offer future training plans. Because all communication and documents are stored in the system, anyone in the company can access the complete customer history at any time.

Benefits of CRM Integration with ERP

- **360° Customer View**: Combine sales, payment, support, and delivery history

- **Improved Sales Efficiency**: Focus on high-value leads with real-time visibility

- **Better Forecasting**: Understand sales trends and pipeline health

- **Stronger Collaboration**: Multiple teams access shared customer insights
- **Increased Retention**: Engage proactively with customers and resolve issues faster

Key CRM Metrics to Track

- Number of leads and conversions
- Sales pipeline value
- Average deal closure time
- Customer satisfaction (CSAT) or Net Promoter Score (NPS)
- Support response and resolution times
- Repeat business ratio

Who Uses the CRM Module?

- **Sales Executives and Managers** – Lead nurturing, follow-ups, forecasting
- **Marketing Teams** – Campaigns, customer segmentation, content targeting
- **Customer Service Teams** – Issue tracking, escalations, service management
- **Leadership** – Performance dashboards, growth trends, and strategic analysis

Common Challenges and How ERP Helps

- **Scattered customer data** – ERP CRM centralizes information
- **Missed follow-ups** – Reminders and task lists keep sales on track
- **Loss of communication history** – Logs and timelines provide full visibility
- **Delayed issue resolution** – Ticketing systems and SLA tracking improve response times

In Summary

Customer Relationship Management in ERP is not just a sales tool—it's a business intelligence system for every team that interacts with customers. From the first email to post-sale support, the CRM module ensures every engagement is timely, informed, and coordinated. Understanding this module enables teams to work more effectively, retain more customers, and improve overall service quality.

In the next chapter, we'll explore **Inventory and Warehouse Management**—how businesses use ERP to monitor stock, track movements, and maintain the delicate balance between availability and cost.

Chapter 19
Inventory and Warehouse Management: Tracking and Controlling Stock with ERP

Inventory is one of the most valuable assets for many businesses—whether you're a retailer, manufacturer, distributor, or service provider. Poor inventory control can lead to overstocking, stockouts, losses, or delays that directly impact profitability and customer satisfaction. An ERP system provides a comprehensive solution to manage inventory and warehouse operations in real time, ensuring accuracy, traceability, and cost control.

This chapter explains how ERP systems manage stock levels, warehouses, movements, and valuation, and how different departments—from procurement to sales to accounts—interact with inventory data to drive smarter business decisions.

What is Inventory Management in ERP?

Inventory management involves tracking the quantity, location, status, and movement of stock across a business. In ERP systems, the **Inventory** or **Stock Module** helps manage:

- Item master data
- Stock availability and movement
- Reorder levels and automatic alerts
- Warehousing and location-based storage
- Batch/serial tracking
- Stock valuation and costing methods

Because ERP integrates inventory with procurement, sales, finance, and manufacturing, all updates are synchronized across departments.

Core Concepts in Inventory Management

1. **Item Master**

   The foundation of inventory tracking is the item master record. It contains:

   - Item code and name
   - Description and specifications
   - Unit of measure (e.g., pieces, kilograms, liters)
   - Default supplier, brand, barcode, and tax codes
   - Reorder level and lead time
   - Costing method (FIFO, LIFO, Weighted Average)

2. **Warehouses and Locations**

   ERP systems allow businesses to define multiple **warehouses, locations**, or **bins**. This supports:

   - Central warehouses and retail branches
   - Raw material vs. finished goods segregation
   - Consignment stock tracking
   - Transit locations for inter-warehouse transfers

3. **Stock Transactions**

   Common inventory movements include:

   - **Stock Receipt**: Goods received from a supplier
   - **Stock Issue**: Goods issued for production or internal use
   - **Delivery**: Items shipped to customers
   - **Return**: Returned items from customers or to suppliers
   - **Transfer**: Movement between warehouses
   - **Adjustment**: Correction of physical stock mismatch
   - Each transaction updates stock levels and creates an audit trail.

4. **Batch and Serial Number Tracking**

For industries like pharma, electronics, or food, ERP supports:

- Batch-wise tracking (expiry dates, manufacturing info)
- Serial numbers for warranty and service tracking
- Barcode or QR code scanning during transactions

5. **Stock Valuation**

Inventory costs affect financial statements and decision-making. ERP systems support multiple valuation methods:

- **FIFO (First In, First Out)**: Oldest inventory used first
- **LIFO (Last In, First Out)**: Newest inventory used first
- **Weighted Average**: Average cost of available stock
- **Standard Costing**: Predefined unit costs

Valuation is updated automatically during purchases, production, and delivery.

Warehouse Operations in ERP

Warehouse functionality ensures that stock movements are accurately recorded, traceable, and efficient. ERP systems allow:

- **Stock Picking and Packing**: Prepare items for delivery based on delivery notes
- **Putaway Strategies**: Assign items to storage locations automatically based on rules
- **Cycle Counting**: Regularly count selected items for accuracy
- **Stock Reconciliation**: Compare physical and system stock levels and adjust as needed

Integration with Other Modules

Inventory in ERP doesn't work in isolation. It interacts closely with:

- **Procurement**: Automatically updates stock when items are received

- **Sales**: Checks availability before confirming orders or deliveries
- **Manufacturing**: Issues raw materials for production and receives finished goods
- **Finance**: Tracks inventory value on the balance sheet and integrates with cost of goods sold (COGS)
- **Projects**: Allocates materials to specific projects or job sites

Real-World Example

A construction company uses ERP to manage cement, tiles, wires, and tools across four warehouses. When a site requests 200 bags of cement, the ERP checks stock at the nearest warehouse. If available, a stock issue is generated. If not, a transfer from the main warehouse is initiated. Each bag is tagged with a batch number. The system automatically adjusts inventory levels and updates the material cost in project reports. At the end of the week, stock reports and alerts help the procurement team reorder supplies before they run out.

Benefits of ERP-Based Inventory Management

- Real-time visibility of stock across locations
- Reduced stockouts and overstocking
- Better inventory forecasting and planning
- Improved warehouse efficiency and accountability
- Streamlined integration with sales, purchasing, and manufacturing
- Minimized losses due to expiry, pilferage, or manual errors

Common Challenges and ERP Solutions

Challenge	ERP-Based Solution
Manual inventory tracking	Barcode/QR scanning and automated stock entries
Stock mismatches	Real-time updates, cycle counts, and audit logs

Delayed reordering	Automated reorder alerts and supplier linkages
Multi-location complexity	Centralized warehouse and transfer management
Valuation discrepancies	System-enforced costing rules and historical tracking

Who Uses the Inventory Module?

- **Warehouse Staff** – Manage receipts, issues, transfers

- **Procurement Officers** – Monitor stock levels and reorder points

- **Sales Teams** – Check availability before confirming orders

- **Accounts and Auditors** – Track inventory value and reconciliations

- **Operations Managers** – Analyze trends and usage efficiency

In Summary

Inventory and warehouse management are crucial for cost control, customer service, and operational continuity. ERP systems provide the tools to track stock accurately, automate replenishment, and ensure that the right materials are available in the right place at the right time. Understanding how inventory functions across the organization helps reduce waste, improve profitability, and support seamless workflows between departments.

In the next chapter, we will focus on **Finance and Accounting in ERP**, explaining how all transactions—from sales to purchases to payroll—are reflected in financial reports and compliance records.

Chapter 20
Finance and Accounting in ERP: Automating Transactions and Enabling Financial Control

Finance is at the core of every business decision. Whether it's managing cash flow, analyzing profitability, tracking expenses, or complying with tax regulations, finance and accounting processes provide the data that drives business direction. ERP systems simplify and automate financial operations by linking accounting with procurement, sales, payroll, inventory, and other modules.

In this chapter, we'll explore how ERP systems handle financial transactions, manage ledgers, support budgeting, and provide accurate, real-time financial reporting.

What is Finance and Accounting in ERP?

The **Finance and Accounting module** in ERP systems manages a company's monetary transactions and ensures compliance with legal and regulatory frameworks. Unlike standalone accounting software, ERP accounting is fully integrated—every transaction in sales, purchase, payroll, or inventory is automatically recorded in the financial system.

Key areas include:

- General ledger and journal entries
- Accounts payable and receivable
- Bank reconciliation
- Tax calculation and compliance
- Asset management
- Financial statements and audit readiness

Core Components of ERP Finance

1. **Chart of Accounts (CoA):** This is the backbone of any accounting system. It defines all the accounts used to categorize transactions (e.g., Sales Revenue, Office Supplies, Bank Accounts, Salaries Expense). A well-structured CoA reflects your business operations and reporting needs.

2. **General Ledger (GL):** The general ledger holds all financial transactions. Each transaction results in a **debit** and **credit** entry to ensure the books are always balanced (double-entry bookkeeping). Examples:

   o A sales invoice creates revenue (credit) and receivable (debit)

   o A purchase invoice creates expense (debit) and payable (credit)

3. **Accounts Receivable (AR) :** Tracks amounts customers owe to the company. Key functions include:

   o Sales invoicing

   o Customer payments

   o Aging reports and dunning letters

82

- ○ Credit limit management

4. **Accounts Payable (AP):** Manages money owed to vendors. The ERP system tracks:

   - ○ Vendor invoices
   - ○ Due dates and early payment discounts
   - ○ Payment schedules
   - ○ Integration with purchase orders and goods receipts

5. **Bank and Cash Management:** ERP systems support:

   - ○ Bank reconciliation
   - ○ Payment vouchers (cheques, bank transfers, online payments)
   - ○ Petty cash handling
   - ○ Multi-currency support and exchange gain/loss calculation

6. **Fixed Asset Management:** Tracks physical assets like equipment, buildings, or vehicles:

   - ○ Acquisition cost and depreciation schedule
   - ○ Asset tagging and location tracking
   - ○ Disposal, transfer, or revaluation
   - ○ Integration with accounting for depreciation expenses

7. **Tax Management:** ERP supports various tax rules and jurisdictions:

   - ○ Automatic calculation of VAT/GST/Sales Tax
   - ○ Tax filing reports
   - ○ Withholding tax management
   - ○ Country-specific compliance formats

Real-World Example

When a company receives a purchase invoice for office furniture, the ERP system:

- Records an expense in the general ledger

- Updates the accounts payable ledger

- Increases fixed asset records if it's a capital expense

- Flags the invoice for payment approval

- Once paid, deducts the amount from the bank account and marks the vendor as paid

All these steps happen in the background without requiring manual entry in each module.

Financial Reporting in ERP

The finance module generates critical reports for internal decision-making and external compliance:

- Profit and Loss Statement

- Balance Sheet

- Cash Flow Statement

- Trial Balance

- Journal Reports

- Tax Returns and Audit Logs

- Budget vs. Actual Reports

Reports can be filtered by department, cost center, project, period, or customer to enable granular financial analysis.

Integration with Other Modules

Module	Finance Integration
Sales	Invoices and customer payments (Accounts Receivable)
Purchase	Vendor bills and payments (Accounts Payable)

Inventory	Stock valuation and COGS entries
Payroll	Salary disbursements, tax deductions, and accruals
Projects	Cost tracking and project-wise profitability
Assets	Depreciation and asset maintenance costing

Because of this integration, financial records are always up to date and accurate, eliminating the delays of disconnected systems.

Key Financial Controls in ERP

- **Role-Based Access**: Restricts who can view or modify financial records
- **Approval Workflows**: Enforces checks before payments or journal entries
- **Audit Trails**: Maintains a log of every change made to financial data
- **Budget Control**: Alerts if spending exceeds predefined budgets
- **Multi-Currency and Consolidation**: Supports global operations with currency conversion and intercompany accounting

Common Challenges and ERP Solutions

Challenge	ERP Solution
Delayed month-end close	Real-time transaction posting and reconciliation
Manual data consolidation	Automated multi-department rollups

Inaccurate reporting	Live dashboards and system-based calculations
Missed payments or follow-ups	Reminders, schedules, and aging reports
Regulatory non-compliance	Built-in tax rules and audit logs

Who Uses the Finance Module?

- **Accountants and Finance Teams** – Record and review transactions

- **CFOs and Controllers** – Monitor financial health and compliance

- **Auditors** – Verify reports, records, and supporting documents

- **Department Heads** – Track budget consumption and financial performance

- **Executive Teams** – Make strategic decisions based on financial KPIs

In Summary

The finance and accounting module is the foundation of ERP systems, offering real-time visibility, control, and automation over a company's financial health. By connecting transactions from across departments, it helps ensure accuracy, compliance, and strategic insight. Understanding how this module works—even at a basic level—is essential for anyone involved in budgeting, reporting, purchasing, or financial decision-making.

In the next chapter, we'll explore **HR and Payroll Systems**, showing how ERP helps manage employee records, salaries, attendance, and leave—integrated with both finance and operations.

Chapter 21
HR and Payroll Systems: Managing People, Payroll, and Productivity in ERP

Employees are the most valuable assets of any organization. Managing their information, attendance, payroll, benefits, and performance requires a systematic and secure approach. ERP systems offer Human Resources (HR) and Payroll modules that bring structure, consistency, and automation to workforce management—reducing administrative effort and ensuring compliance with labor laws and company policies.

In this chapter, we'll explore how ERP systems support HR operations from recruitment to retirement, and how payroll is processed with accuracy, transparency, and integration with finance and compliance modules.

What Are HR and Payroll Modules in ERP?

The **HR module** in an ERP system manages employee data, attendance, leaves, appraisals, training, and organizational structure. The **Payroll module** handles salary calculations, tax deductions, statutory benefits, and payslip generation.

When integrated, these modules eliminate duplication, ensure policy consistency, and align workforce planning with financial and operational strategies.

Core Components of the HR Module

1. **Employee Master Records**

   Each employee has a digital profile that includes:

   ○ Personal details (name, contact, ID, nationality)

   ○ Job information (designation, department, supervisor, joining date)

   ○ Compensation and benefits

   ○ Documents (contracts, certifications, IDs)

   ○ Emergency contacts and dependents

2. Organizational Structure

ERP allows definition of departments, cost centers, job roles, and reporting hierarchies, enabling:

○ Proper workflow routing

○ Department-level budgeting and headcount planning

○ Role-based access controls

3. Attendance and Leave Management

Employees can mark attendance via:

○ Manual input

○ Biometric devices or swipe cards (integrated with ERP)

○ Remote attendance with location tagging

4. Leave types (sick, annual, unpaid, etc.) are tracked with:

○ Leave balance calculation

○ Holiday calendars

○ Leave approval workflows

○ Auto carry-forward rules

5. Performance and Appraisals

ERP-based appraisal systems support:

○ Goal setting and KPI tracking

○ Peer and manager reviews

○ Appraisal cycles and rating history

○ Salary revision based on performance

6. Training and Development

Track employee training programs, certifications, course completion, and future learning needs.

7. Exit and Separation

Resignation, clearance, final settlement, and exit interviews can be managed through the ERP.

Core Components of the Payroll Module

1. **Salary Structures and Components**

   Define earnings (basic, allowances, overtime) and deductions (tax, provident fund, loans). The system supports:

   o   Multiple salary slabs

   o   Role-based structures

   o   Hourly, daily, or monthly wages

2. **Payroll Processing**

   o   Auto calculation of gross salary, deductions, and net pay

   o   Integration with attendance, leaves, and overtime

   o   Batch processing for departments or the whole organization

   o   Payslip generation and distribution via email or portal

3. **Tax and Compliance**

   o   Automatic TDS (Tax Deducted at Source) calculation

   o   Provident Fund, Social Security, and other statutory deductions

   o   Generation of tax forms and compliance reports

   o   Year-end summaries for employees

4. **Loans and Advances**

   ERP can manage employee loans with:

   o   Repayment schedules

   o   Interest calculations

   o   Auto-deductions from salary

5. **Bank Payments**

   Salary payments can be processed via:

- ○ Bank file generation (for upload to corporate banking platforms)
- ○ Direct integration with payroll banks (where supported)

Real-World Example

A logistics company uses ERP to manage over 500 employees. Each staff member clocks in using biometric devices integrated with the HR module. Monthly attendance is automatically pulled into the payroll engine. Salaries are calculated based on structure, overtime, and deductions. The finance team reviews the final payroll, and payslips are emailed to employees. Year-end tax forms are also auto-generated from the system.

Benefits of HR and Payroll in ERP

- Centralized employee data with secure access
- Reduced paperwork and manual calculation errors
- Transparent payroll processing with audit trails
- Real-time visibility into attendance, leaves, and headcount
- Easier compliance with labor laws and tax regulations
- Enhanced employee satisfaction with self-service portals

Self-Service Portals

Modern ERP systems offer employee and manager self-service features:

- Apply for leave
- Download payslips
- Update contact details
- View appraisal results
- Submit travel or expense claims
- These features reduce HR workload and improve transparency.

Integration with Other Modules

Module	HR/Payroll Interaction
Finance	Salary accounting, reimbursements, tax filing
Projects	Allocate staff time and effort to specific projects
Attendance	Link biometric data for payroll accuracy
Asset Management	Assign laptops, vehicles, or tools to employees
Recruitment	Transfer candidate data to employee records

Common Challenges and ERP Solutions

Challenge	ERP Solution
Manual payroll calculations	Automated salary processing and error checking
Leave balance confusion	Real-time leave balance tracking and reporting
Lack of compliance tracking	Built-in tax rules, PF/ESI/SSO automation
HR data scattered in files	Centralized, searchable employee database
Late salary disbursement	Scheduled, system-driven payroll calendar

Who Uses the HR and Payroll Module?

- **HR Managers** – Maintain records, policies, and approvals

- **Payroll Officers** – Handle calculations, taxes, and payments

- **Finance Team** – Reconcile payroll entries and plan budgets

- **Department Heads** – Approve leaves, monitor team performance

- **Employees** – Access self-service functions and update profiles

Transform HR Operations with ERPNext: Automate Employee Management, Streamline Leave & Attendance, Enhance Performance lms.syncbricks.com	

In Summary

HR and payroll management in ERP systems transforms complex and sensitive people operations into efficient, compliant, and transparent workflows. By integrating employee data with time, attendance, finance, and performance, ERP enables organizations to manage human capital more strategically. Whether you're in HR, finance, or team leadership, understanding this module helps foster accountability, accuracy, and employee satisfaction.

In the next chapter, we will explore how ERP systems support **Projects, Manufacturing, and Service Management**, helping businesses plan, execute, and track work in structured and profitable ways.

Chapter 22
Projects, Manufacturing, and Service Management in ERP: Streamlining Work Execution Across Business Models

ERP systems are not just for managing sales, purchases, and accounting—they also support operational workflows like project management, manufacturing processes, and after-sales service. These modules help businesses plan work, allocate resources, track progress, and monitor costs across a wide variety of industries, from construction and engineering to factories and field services.

This chapter provides an overview of how modern ERP systems help manage projects, production, and service operations in an integrated, efficient, and data-driven manner.

Project Management in ERP

ERP systems often include a **Projects module** designed for organizations involved in client services, construction, consulting, software development, or internal strategic initiatives.

Key Features:

1. **Project Creation and Planning**

   o Define project name, client, start/end dates, milestones, and assigned team members

   o Set project type (internal, external, billable)

   o Link to a sales order, contract, or cost center

2. **Task Management and Scheduling**

   o Break projects into tasks or phases

   o Assign deadlines and responsibilities

   o Use Gantt charts or Kanban views for visualization

   o Set dependencies between tasks

3. **Time and Expense Tracking**

   ○ Employees can log hours against tasks

   ○ Track billable vs. non-billable time

   ○ Capture expenses (travel, materials) linked to the project

4. **Budget and Cost Tracking**

   ○ Estimate budgets for labor, materials, and subcontractors

   ○ Compare planned vs. actual costs

   ○ Monitor project profitability in real time

5. **Invoicing and Billing**

   ○ Create project-based invoices (milestone, time & materials, fixed price)

   ○ Automate billing based on hours or completion percentage

Real-World Example:

A consultancy firm uses the ERP project module to manage a digital transformation engagement for a client. Tasks are assigned to team members, who log hours each week. Monthly invoices are auto-generated based on approved timesheets. Project dashboards show time utilization, cost-to-completion, and revenue projections.

Manufacturing and Production in ERP

Manufacturing companies use ERP systems to plan, execute, and track production orders—ensuring that raw materials are converted into finished goods efficiently and cost-effectively.

Key Manufacturing Functions:

1. **Bill of Materials (BOM)**

   ○ Defines the components and quantities required to manufacture a product

   ○ Can include sub-assemblies and alternative items

   ○ Links directly to inventory for raw material planning

2. Work Orders / Job Cards

- Authorize production for a specific quantity
- Assign machines, shifts, and operators
- Track status (Not Started, In Progress, Completed)

3. Material Requirement Planning (MRP)

- Automatically calculates material needs based on BOM and production plans
- Generates procurement and stock transfer suggestions
- Ensures optimal inventory without overstocking

4. Shop Floor Management

- Record real-time progress of jobs
- Track output, scrap, downtime, and worker efficiency
- Support barcode-based work tracking

5. Costing and Valuation

- Calculate per-unit production cost based on materials, labor, and overheads
- Track variances between estimated and actual costs
- Update inventory value upon completion

Real-World Example:

A furniture manufacturer uses ERP to manage production of custom tables. When a customer order is confirmed, a work order is generated. The system checks the BOM, reserves materials, and schedules the job. After production, finished items are transferred to inventory, and labor time is logged for costing. Invoices are issued automatically.

Service Management in ERP

Service-oriented businesses—like IT support companies, equipment rental providers, or facilities management firms—benefit from ERP modules that manage service delivery, tracking, and billing.

Key Functions:

1. **Service Orders / Requests**

   o   Track requests for maintenance, repair, or installation

   o   Assign field technicians or service teams

   o   Monitor resolution time and service-level agreements (SLAs)

2. **Asset Management**

   o   Maintain a registry of equipment or client-owned assets

   o   Schedule preventive maintenance

   o   Record service history and warranty information

3. **Service Contracts and Warranties**

   o   Manage annual maintenance contracts (AMCs)

   o   Track service entitlements and coverage periods

   o   Link with customer invoicing and renewals

4. **Mobile Access and Field Updates**

   o   Allow service staff to update jobs via tablets or smartphones

   o   Capture client signatures, photos, and parts used on-site

   o   Generate service reports immediately

5. **Service Invoicing and Feedback**

   o   Bill for time, parts, or fixed services

   o   Collect customer feedback and ratings

   o   Maintain customer satisfaction history

Real-World Example:

An HVAC company provides AC maintenance across multiple buildings. Each visit is logged in the ERP with location, technician, and parts used. Maintenance schedules are set based on contract frequency. Service teams receive mobile alerts, and clients receive automatic reminders and reports. Billing and performance metrics are fully integrated with the system.

Why ERP Integration Matters

When projects, manufacturing, and service management are part of the ERP system, they integrate seamlessly with:

- **Inventory** – for material tracking
- **HR** – for resource assignment and payroll
- **Sales** – for linking work to client orders
- **Finance** – for real-time cost, revenue, and profitability tracking
- **CRM** – for client communication and service follow-up

This eliminates data silos, improves coordination, and enhances the accuracy of planning and reporting.

In Summary

ERP systems help businesses execute and manage complex operational workflows—whether it's delivering a consulting project, manufacturing a product, or servicing equipment in the field. These modules enable cross-functional teams to collaborate in real time, control costs, deliver on time, and keep customers informed. Understanding these ERP capabilities is especially important for operations, project managers, production heads, and service coordinators.

In the next chapter, we'll cover **ERP Integration and Reporting**, exploring how ERP systems bring everything together through dashboards, cross-module reports, and custom analytics.

Chapter 23
ERP Integration and Reporting: Connecting the Dots Across the Business

One of the most powerful features of an ERP system is its ability to integrate all business functions into a single platform. Unlike standalone tools or disconnected spreadsheets, ERP systems ensure that data flows seamlessly across departments—removing duplication, improving accuracy, and enabling real-time decision-making.

This chapter explores how ERP integration works, how it enhances organizational visibility, and how users can generate meaningful reports and dashboards from different modules to drive business performance.

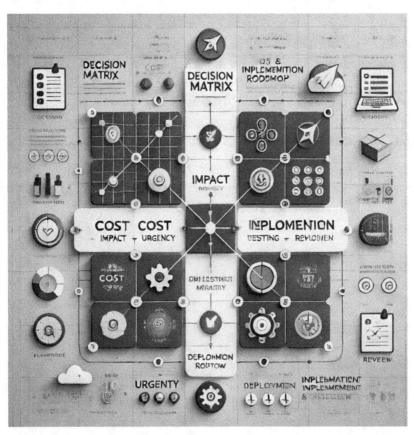

What Is ERP Integration?

ERP integration refers to the seamless connection between different modules within the system—such as sales, finance, HR, inventory, and manufacturing—so that information flows automatically and consistently from one function to another.

Rather than having to manually export data or re-enter it in multiple systems, ERP integration ensures that:

- A customer created in CRM is instantly available to the finance team for invoicing

- A purchase order automatically updates stock and accounts payable

- A project timesheet feeds directly into payroll and billing

- A delivery note reduces inventory and triggers revenue recognition

This level of interconnectivity minimizes errors, speeds up operations, and enables collaboration between teams using shared data.

Examples of ERP Integration in Action

1. **Sales to Finance**

   When a sales order is delivered, the system automatically generates a sales invoice. This invoice updates:

   - Accounts receivable in the finance module

   - Customer ledger and aging reports

   - Revenue recognition entries for financial reporting

2. **Procurement to Inventory and Accounts**

   Upon receipt of goods:

   - Inventory quantities increase in real time

   - A goods receipt note is created

   - A payable entry is logged in the finance module

   - Purchase cost is linked to projects or departments

3. **HR to Payroll and Finance**

   ○ Approved leave, overtime, and attendance logs are used to calculate salaries

   ○ Payroll journals are posted directly into the accounting system

   ○ Employee reimbursements are processed through accounts payable

4. **Manufacturing to Stock and Costing**

   ○ When a work order is completed, finished goods are added to stock

   ○ Raw material consumption is recorded

   ○ Production costs are captured and compared with estimates

   ○ Cost of Goods Sold (COGS) is calculated for financial analysis

What Is ERP Reporting?

ERP reporting involves extracting and presenting data from across the ERP system in structured formats—such as tables, charts, graphs, and dashboards—for decision-making, analysis, and compliance.

Types of reports include:

- **Operational Reports**: Daily sales, delivery schedules, stock levels

- **Financial Reports**: Income statements, balance sheets, trial balances

- **Statutory Reports**: Tax summaries, labor filings, audit logs

- **Analytical Reports**: Sales trends, customer behavior, project profitability

Key Reporting Features in ERP Systems

1. **Custom Report Builders**

   Users can select fields, filters, and conditions to build reports specific to their needs—without writing code.

2. Standard Pre-Built Reports

ERP systems come with templates like:

○ Sales Order Summary

○ Purchase Register

○ Aged Receivables and Payables

○ Employee Attendance Logs

○ Inventory Valuation Reports

3. Dashboards and KPIs

Visual dashboards display key performance indicators (KPIs) such as:

○ Daily revenue

○ Stock turnover

○ Budget vs. actual spending

○ Customer satisfaction ratings

4. Dashboards are often personalized by role—sales reps, accountants, HR managers, and executives can each have their own view.

5. Export and Scheduling Options

Reports can usually be exported in formats like PDF, Excel, or CSV, and scheduled to be emailed at regular intervals.

6. Permission-Based Access

Users only see data they're authorized to access. For example, an HR officer can't view financial reports unless explicitly granted permission.

Benefits of ERP Integration and Reporting

- **Real-Time Decision-Making**: No need to wait for monthly reports—data is always current

- **Cross-Functional Visibility**: Sales, operations, and finance teams work with the same information

- **Error Reduction**: Data entered once is reused consistently, avoiding re-entry mistakes
- **Time Savings**: Automated reporting replaces hours of manual data consolidation
- **Audit Readiness**: All transactions are traceable and documented, easing internal or external audits

Who Uses ERP Reporting?

- **Executives** – Monitor company-wide KPIs and financial health
- **Managers** – Track department performance, employee utilization, or project budgets
- **Accountants** – Prepare compliance reports and reconciliations
- **Sales Teams** – Review pipeline, win/loss ratios, and territory performance
- **Operations Teams** – Monitor stock levels, delivery delays, and production outputs

Common Reporting Challenges Solved by ERP

Challenge	ERP Solution
Delayed or outdated reports	Real-time dashboards with live data
Multiple versions of the same data	Centralized, integrated data repository
Difficulty in customizing reports	User-friendly report builders with filter options
Lack of visibility across functions	Cross-module reports with drill-down capabilities

Real-World Example

A CFO reviews a monthly dashboard showing sales by region, profit margins by product category, overdue receivables, and cash position. With just a few clicks, they can drill down into specific customer accounts or analyze why a product line underperformed. At the same time, the sales manager uses a similar dashboard to review performance against targets and adjust strategy for the next quarter.

Both are working from the same source of truth—thanks to integrated ERP reporting.

In Summary

ERP integration and reporting give organizations a unified view of their business operations. When all modules share data, teams collaborate more effectively, decisions are made faster, and mistakes are minimized. The reporting tools within ERP systems transform raw data into actionable insights, ensuring that the right people have access to the right information at the right time.

In the next chapter, we'll wrap up the ERP section with a guide to **Choosing and Implementing ERP Systems**, offering practical steps and best practices for businesses evaluating or upgrading their ERP platforms.

Chapter 24

Choosing and Implementing ERP Systems: A Practical Guide for Business Leaders

Selecting and implementing an ERP system is one of the most critical decisions a business can make. When done right, ERP brings structure, efficiency, visibility, and growth potential. When done poorly, it can result in cost overruns, employee frustration, and operational setbacks. Whether you're a startup, a growing SME, or an established enterprise, the ERP you choose—and how you implement it—will impact your business for years to come.

This chapter walks through the essential considerations when evaluating ERP options, planning an implementation, and managing the change across your organization.

Why ERP Selection Matters

ERP is not just a software purchase—it's a long-term business transformation initiative. The right system aligns with your business processes, scales with your growth, and integrates with your existing tools. The wrong system creates silos, forces process changes that don't fit your operations, and may become a burden rather than a benefit.

ERP selection should be a strategic, cross-functional decision involving stakeholders from IT, finance, operations, HR, sales, and leadership.

Key Criteria for Choosing an ERP System

1. Business Requirements Fit

Start by identifying what your business needs. Do you need strong inventory management? Complex manufacturing flows? Multi-company accounting? Make sure the ERP supports your core processes out of the box.

2. Scalability and Flexibility

Can the ERP grow with your business? Will it support more users, multi-location operations, or new modules as needed?

3. **Cloud vs. On-Premise**

   Cloud-based ERPs offer flexibility, accessibility, and reduced infrastructure management. On-premise systems offer more control and data ownership. Hybrid models are also common.

4. **Ease of Use**

   The user interface should be intuitive. A system that's hard to learn will result in poor adoption.

5. **Integration Capabilities**

   Can the ERP connect with your existing tools—CRM, ecommerce, payroll systems, or business intelligence platforms?

6. **Support and Vendor Reputation**

   Look at vendor experience, community support, documentation, training resources, and customer service responsiveness.

7. **Customization and Workflow Automation**

   How easy is it to customize the system? Can non-technical users build workflows, set up notifications, and create reports?

8. **Cost and Licensing Model**

   Understand all costs: licensing, implementation, support, upgrades, and hidden fees. Choose between subscription-based pricing and perpetual licensing based on your budget and cash flow.

Popular ERP Systems (and Use Cases)

ERP System	Best For
SAP Business One	Medium to large enterprises with complex processes
Oracle NetSuite	Cloud-first enterprises and global operations

105

Microsoft Dynamics 365	Businesses using Microsoft ecosystem
Odoo	SMEs needing modular, open-source ERP
ERPNext	Startups, services, manufacturers with customization needs
Zoho ERP	Businesses already using Zoho products

There is no one-size-fits-all solution. Select based on your size, industry, budget, and technical maturity.

The ERP Implementation Process

1. **Project Planning and Team Formation**
   - Define goals and scope
   - Assign a cross-functional team
   - Set a timeline and communication plan

2. **Business Process Mapping**
   - Document how things currently work
   - Identify gaps, inefficiencies, and improvement areas
   - Decide which processes should be changed or retained

3. **System Configuration and Customization**
   - Set up users, roles, and permissions
   - Configure modules to match your workflows
   - Customize forms, fields, and approval flows as needed

4. **Data Migration**
   - Clean up existing data
   - Migrate customer records, inventory, financials, vendors, employees

o   Validate data accuracy post-migration

5. **Training and User Adoption**

o   Conduct workshops and hands-on sessions

o   Create cheat sheets, video tutorials, or FAQs

o   Encourage feedback and provide helpdesk support

6. **Testing and Go-Live**

o   Perform UAT (User Acceptance Testing)

o   Simulate real-world transactions

o   Resolve bugs before going live

o   Plan a phased rollout or big bang approach

7. **Post-Implementation Support**

o   Monitor system performance and user activity

o   Address issues quickly

o   Schedule reviews and system updates regularly

Common ERP Implementation Mistakes to Avoid

- **Lack of stakeholder involvement**: Leads to missed requirements and poor adoption

- **Over-customization**: Increases complexity and upgrade challenges

- **Skipping process alignment**: Trying to automate bad processes leads to failure

- **Underestimating training**: Employees need time and support to learn the system

- **No change management**: Resistance to change can derail the project

Tips for a Successful ERP Implementation

- Start small—focus on core modules, then expand

- Involve end-users early to gain buy-in

- Communicate continuously and transparently

- Align the system with how your business works, not the other way around

- Build internal champions—people who understand both the system and your business

A Comprehensive Guide to Mastering ERPNext: Installation, Configuration, Integration, Backup, and Advanced Concepts	

In Summary

Choosing and implementing an ERP system is a journey that transforms how your organization works. A well-selected ERP, implemented thoughtfully, becomes the digital backbone of your company—enabling efficiency, accountability, scalability, and growth. This chapter concludes the ERP section of the book. In the next part, we'll move into **Business Intelligence and Reporting**, exploring how organizations turn ERP data into insights and decisions.

Excellent, we're now entering **Part 5: Business Intelligence and Reporting**, where the focus shifts from process execution to insight and decision-making. Let's begin with the first chapter in this part.

PART 5

BUSINESS INTELLIGENCE AND REPORTING

Chapter 25
Introduction to Business Intelligence: Turning Data into Actionable Insights

In today's digital workplace, data is everywhere. Every transaction, interaction, and activity—whether it's a sale, a support call, or a stock adjustment—creates data. But without the ability to make sense of this data, it's just digital noise. **Business Intelligence (BI)** is the discipline that transforms raw data into meaningful insights, helping professionals make informed decisions and solve problems faster.

In this chapter, we explore what BI is, why it matters across roles, and how organizations use BI to stay competitive, agile, and customer-focused.

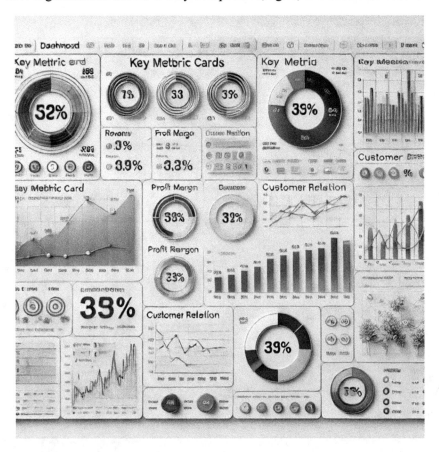

What is Business Intelligence?

Business Intelligence is a set of tools, technologies, and practices that analyze business data and present it in a visual, understandable way. It helps people at all levels of an organization:

- Understand what's happening in the business
- Track performance and results over time
- Identify trends, risks, and opportunities
- Make evidence-based decisions rather than assumptions

Unlike traditional reports, which often come in static, delayed formats, BI provides real-time, interactive dashboards and reports that anyone can explore and interpret.

The Evolution of BI in Business

Traditionally, only senior executives or data analysts had access to business reports—often delivered days or weeks after the events they described. Today, BI tools allow employees, managers, and executives to explore up-to-date information themselves. This democratization of data is known as **self-service BI**.

Examples of common BI use:

- A sales manager reviewing monthly performance across regions
- A finance officer monitoring expense trends
- A warehouse team tracking slow-moving stock
- A CEO looking at profitability dashboards before a board meeting

Key Components of a BI System

1. **Data Sources**
2. BI pulls data from systems like ERP, CRM, accounting, HR, website analytics, and more.
3. **Data Modeling and ETL**
4. ETL (Extract, Transform, Load) processes clean and organize data into a structure suitable for reporting.

5. Data Warehouse / Data Mart

6. A centralized repository where processed data is stored for analysis. Some tools use live connections instead.

7. Visualization Tools

8. Software that displays data in charts, graphs, maps, tables, and dashboards.

9. Reports and Dashboards

10. Interactive, visual summaries of key business metrics and performance indicators.

Why BI Matters in Every Department

Department	BI Use Case
Sales	Analyze top-selling products, conversion rates, revenue per region
Marketing	Track campaign performance, website traffic, lead generation
Finance	Monitor budgets, cash flow, profit margins, and forecasts
Operations	Optimize inventory, delivery times, supplier performance
HR	Review employee turnover, training ROI, recruitment trends
Customer Service	Measure response time, ticket resolution, satisfaction scores

Regardless of industry or role, BI empowers teams to work smarter.

Real-World Example

A retail company uses BI dashboards to track hourly sales across stores. One store is consistently underperforming. Upon drilling into the data, they notice fewer footfalls and higher return rates. The store manager investigates and finds a staffing issue during peak hours. Adjustments are made, and within a month, performance improves. This level of visibility and responsiveness wouldn't be possible with traditional monthly reports.

Benefits of Implementing BI

- **Faster decisions** with live data
- **Greater accuracy** by reducing manual reporting errors
- **Improved collaboration** through shared data views
- **Better performance tracking** with real-time KPIs
- **Early risk detection** through alerts and trends
- **Increased accountability** across teams and functions

In Summary

Business Intelligence is more than just charts and dashboards—it's a mindset shift. It helps organizations move from reactive decision-making to proactive management. Whether you're leading a team or working on the front lines, understanding and using BI tools helps you measure impact, discover insights, and contribute strategically to your organization.

In the next chapter, we'll explore **Dashboards, KPIs, and Reporting Types**—diving deeper into how BI presents data and which types of reports every professional should understand.

Chapter 26
Dashboards, KPIs, and Reporting Types: Visualizing What Matters Most

The core purpose of Business Intelligence (BI) is to help people make better decisions—and to do that effectively, data must be presented in a format that is easy to understand and act on. This is where dashboards, key performance indicators (KPIs), and different types of reports play a vital role.

In this chapter, we will explore how dashboards are used in modern workplaces, how KPIs are defined and monitored, and the various types of reports commonly used in business operations.

What Is a Dashboard?

A **dashboard** is a visual display of important metrics and data points arranged in a single view. Think of it as a car dashboard—but for your business. Just like a car dashboard shows speed, fuel, and engine health, a business dashboard shows sales, profit margins, customer satisfaction, or inventory levels—all at a glance.

Dashboards allow users to:

- Monitor live data from multiple systems

- Spot trends or anomalies instantly

- Drill down into specific areas for deeper insights

- Make faster, evidence-based decisions

Types of Dashboards

1. **Operational Dashboards**

   o Used by front-line teams to monitor day-to-day activities

   o Examples: daily sales figures, inventory movement, support ticket status

2. **Analytical Dashboards**

   - Used to explore trends, patterns, and performance over time

   - Examples: monthly revenue growth, customer churn rate, campaign analysis

3. **Strategic Dashboards**

   - Used by executives for long-term planning and decision-making

   - Examples: company-wide profitability, market expansion performance, annual goals tracking

4. **Functional Dashboards**

   - Focused on specific departments or functions

   - Examples: HR dashboard for leave trends, finance dashboard for cash flow

Understanding KPIs (Key Performance Indicators)

A **KPI** is a measurable value that shows how effectively a person, team, or company is achieving a key business objective. KPIs should be specific, relevant, and actionable.

Characteristics of a Good KPI:

- **Clear**: Everyone understands what it measures

- **Relevant**: Aligned with business goals

- **Measurable**: Based on real, available data

- **Time-bound**: Tracked over a defined period

- **Actionable**: Provides insight that can drive decisions

Examples of Common KPIs:

Area	KPI Example
Sales	Monthly sales growth, conversion rate
Finance	Net profit margin, accounts receivable aging
Operations	On-time delivery rate, production uptime
Marketing	Cost per lead, email open rate
Customer Service	First response time, ticket resolution rate
HR	Employee turnover, training completion rate

Each department may have different KPIs, but they all contribute to the organization's strategic goals.

Types of Reports in BI

While dashboards give a high-level view, **reports** provide more detailed, structured insights. Different reporting types serve different business needs.

1. **Summary Reports**
   - Provide a high-level overview of key metrics
   - Example: Weekly sales performance by region

2. **Detail Reports**
   - Contain granular data with itemized records
   - Example: List of every sales invoice with date, amount, and customer

3. **Trend Reports**
   - Show data over time to identify patterns
   - Example: Customer acquisition trends over the past 12 months

4. **Exception Reports**
   - Highlight deviations from expected results
   - Example: Products with zero sales in the last quarter

5. **Comparative Reports**
   - Compare performance across time periods, teams, or geographies
   - Example: Departmental expense comparison between Q1 and Q2

6. **Interactive Reports**
   - Allow users to apply filters, drill down, or change views
   - Example: A dashboard where the user can select a region to view localized metrics

Real-World Example

An ecommerce manager opens the company's BI dashboard every morning. At the top, she sees:

- Total orders today (operational KPI)
- Sales vs. target for the month (strategic KPI)
- Average cart value and return rate (analytical KPIs)

By 10:00 a.m., she notices a spike in product returns. She drills down into the report and finds that a specific batch of products from one supplier has higher-than-usual complaints. The purchasing team is notified immediately, avoiding further losses.

This quick detection and response are only possible because dashboards and reports are available in real time.

Best Practices for Dashboards and Reporting

- **Keep it simple**: Don't overload the dashboard—focus on critical metrics

- **Use visual cues**: Colors, icons, and charts improve readability

- **Enable drill-down**: Let users explore the details behind the numbers

- **Automate updates**: Ensure data refreshes on schedule (hourly, daily, etc.)

- **Validate data sources**: Inaccurate data leads to poor decisions

- **Customize by role**: Tailor dashboards for each team's specific needs

In Summary

Dashboards, KPIs, and reports are not just tools for analysts—they are everyday essentials for modern professionals. When designed well, they turn raw data into visual narratives that support better thinking and faster action. Understanding how to read and build effective dashboards makes you a more informed, efficient, and valuable contributor to any organization.

In the next chapter, we'll examine the tools that power modern BI—specifically **Power BI, Tableau, and Google Data Studio**—and how they can be applied in real-world business scenarios.

Chapter 27
BI Tools: Power BI, Tableau, and Google Data Studio

Business Intelligence (BI) tools are the engines that turn raw data into insights. While ERP systems often come with built-in reporting tools, modern organizations rely on dedicated BI platforms to visualize complex data across multiple systems—sales, marketing, finance, operations, customer service, and more.

This chapter introduces three of the most widely used BI tools—**Power BI**, **Tableau**, and **Google Data Studio**—explaining their strengths, typical use cases, and suitability for different roles and business sizes.

What Makes a BI Tool Powerful?

An effective BI tool should:

- Connect to multiple data sources (ERP, spreadsheets, databases, cloud apps)

- Clean and transform data into usable formats

- Build interactive dashboards and reports

- Allow filtering, slicing, and drilling into data

- Share insights securely with teams and decision-makers

All three tools discussed here meet these criteria, but they differ in design philosophy, pricing, and user experience.

1. Microsoft Power BI

Overview:

Power BI is a Microsoft product designed for business users. It integrates well with Excel, Microsoft 365, and Azure services, making it a popular choice among companies using the Microsoft ecosystem.

Key Features:

- Drag-and-drop interface for dashboard building

- Connects to Excel, SQL databases, SharePoint, ERP systems, cloud platforms
- Power Query for data transformation
- DAX (Data Analysis Expressions) language for advanced formulas
- Row-level security for data protection
- Power BI Service for online dashboard sharing
- Mobile app for viewing reports on the go

Best For:

- Medium to large organizations
- Financial analysts, sales managers, department heads
- Anyone already using Microsoft Excel or Office 365

Example Use Case:

A retail chain connects its ERP sales data, foot traffic counters, and marketing campaign results into Power BI to monitor store performance in real time.

Master Microsoft Power BI Unlock the power of data analytics and visualization with Power BI. lms.syncbricks.com	

2. Tableau

Overview:

Tableau is a leading visual analytics platform known for its powerful data exploration and visualization capabilities. It's widely used in industries like healthcare, banking, and academia where deep analytical insights are essential.

Key Features:

- Highly interactive and customizable visualizations
- Powerful for exploratory data analysis
- Connects to hundreds of data sources (cloud, local, big data platforms)
- Tableau Prep for data cleaning and transformation
- Real-time dashboard interactivity
- Extensive community and online resources

Best For:

- Data analysts and business intelligence teams
- Organizations needing advanced visual storytelling
- Scenarios with very large or complex datasets

Example Use Case:

A logistics company uses Tableau to analyze delivery performance across regions, monitor on-time rates, and visualize bottlenecks by hub.

3. Google Data Studio (Now Looker Studio)

Overview:

Google Data Studio—now known as **Looker Studio**—is a free cloud-based BI tool that integrates easily with Google products like Sheets, Analytics, Ads, and BigQuery. It is ideal for startups, marketers, and small businesses looking for simple yet powerful reporting.

Key Features:

- Free to use with Google account
- Easy integration with Google Analytics, Ads, YouTube, and Sheets
- Templates for marketing and web traffic dashboards
- Live reports with sharing and collaboration features

- No installation—100% cloud-based

Best For:

- Digital marketing teams
- Small businesses
- Google Workspace users

Example Use Case:

A digital agency builds client dashboards showing web traffic, campaign ROI, and social media reach using Google Analytics and Ads data.

Comparison Summary

Feature / Tool	Power BI	Tableau	Google Data Studio
Platform	Microsoft	Salesforce (Tableau)	Google (Free)
Ease of Use	Easy for Excel users	Steeper learning curve	Very easy for beginners
Pricing	Affordable (Pro license)	Premium pricing	Free
Data Sources	Very broad	Very broad	Limited to popular sources
Offline Use	Supported (Power BI Desktop)	Supported (Tableau Desktop)	Not supported (cloud only)
Best Use Case	Corporate BI, finance	Advanced analytics, big data	Marketing, startups

How to Choose the Right BI Tool

- **If you already use Microsoft Excel and Office 365**, Power BI is a natural fit.

- **If your focus is on advanced visual storytelling or you manage complex datasets**, Tableau is a better option.

- **If you're running a small business or digital campaigns**, Google Data Studio offers a low-barrier entry to BI.

Ultimately, your choice should depend on your technical capacity, integration needs, and the complexity of your reporting requirements.

In Summary

Power BI, Tableau, and Google Data Studio each offer powerful capabilities for turning data into insight. While they differ in complexity, pricing, and ecosystem alignment, they all help organizations build clarity, monitor performance, and empower teams to act on data. Learning any of these tools—especially at a basic level—is a valuable skill for professionals across departments.

In the next chapter, we'll explore **Data-Driven Decision Making**—how organizations shift from intuition-based decisions to insight-driven strategies using BI and analytics.

Chapter 28
Data-Driven Decision Making: Moving from Gut Feelings to Informed Actions

In today's competitive environment, organizations that make decisions based on data outperform those that rely on guesswork, tradition, or intuition. This shift—known as **Data-Driven Decision Making (DDDM)**—is not just about using reports or dashboards. It's about embedding a culture where decisions at every level are supported by evidence.

In this chapter, we explore what it means to be data-driven, how it changes the way organizations think and act, and how professionals at any level can apply this mindset in their daily work.

What Is Data-Driven Decision Making?

Data-driven decision making is the practice of using objective data—collected, processed, and analyzed—to guide business choices. Rather than relying solely on experience or instinct, a data-driven organization asks:

- What does the data say?
- What trend or pattern is emerging?
- What are the measurable outcomes of our decisions?

This approach reduces bias, increases transparency, and leads to more consistent and justifiable decisions.

Why Data-Driven Thinking Matters

Imagine a marketing manager launching a new campaign. In a traditional approach, they might rely on past experience or anecdotal feedback. In a data-driven approach, they examine click-through rates, audience segments, previous ROI, and user behavior trends before launching—and then adjust based on real-time results.

Whether it's deciding where to open a new store, which supplier to work with, or which employees to promote, using data leads to better outcomes.

Benefits of Data-Driven Decision Making

1. **Improved Accuracy**
2. Decisions are based on facts, not assumptions or hearsay.
3. **Faster Problem Solving**
4. Root causes are identified more quickly with the help of data.
5. **More Accountability**
6. When decisions are made transparently with data, everyone is clear about what was done and why.
7. **Greater Innovation**
8. Data reveals patterns and opportunities that might otherwise be overlooked.
9. **Continuous Improvement**
10. Performance can be measured, compared, and optimized over time.

Common Areas Where Data Guides Decisions

Function	Example Decisions Based on Data
Sales	Which region or product line to focus on next quarter
Marketing	Which channel brings the most qualified leads
Finance	Where cost-cutting will impact margins the least
HR	Which roles have the highest turnover and why
Customer Service	When and where service response times are lagging
Operations	Which suppliers deliver consistently on time

Real-World Example

A manufacturing company was experiencing delays in customer deliveries. The operations team assumed the issue was with transportation. However, a review of ERP and BI data showed the problem was upstream—raw material orders were being placed late due to manual approvals. After implementing automated reorder alerts and streamlining the purchase approval process, on-time deliveries improved by 30% in two months.

This improvement wasn't the result of brainstorming or luck—it was the result of following the data trail.

The Role of BI Tools in Decision Making

Business Intelligence tools like Power BI, Tableau, or Google Data Studio help:

- Visualize complex data clearly
- Spot trends and outliers quickly
- Compare performance across teams, regions, or products
- Drill down from high-level metrics into detailed records
- Share insights easily across the organization

With the right dashboards in place, decisions that once took weeks of meetings and reports can now be made in minutes.

Challenges to Becoming Data-Driven

1. **Data Silos**
2. If departments store data separately, insights are incomplete.
3. **Poor Data Quality**
4. Inaccurate or outdated data leads to wrong conclusions.
5. **Lack of Skills**
6. Team members may not know how to interpret or question the data.
7. **Cultural Resistance**
8. People may be uncomfortable challenging long-held practices or assumptions.

9. Overreliance on Data Alone

10. Data supports judgment—it doesn't replace it. Human experience and context are still essential.

Tips for Making Better Data-Driven Decisions

- **Start with a question**: What do you want to know? What decision are you trying to make?

- **Use the right data**: Make sure your data is relevant, recent, and trustworthy.

- **Visualize results**: Use charts or dashboards to simplify interpretation.

- **Collaborate**: Share findings with others to get diverse perspectives.

- **Act, then measure**: Implement changes and track the impact to learn and improve.

- **Train your team**: Build data literacy across the organization.

In Summary

Data-driven decision making empowers professionals to move beyond instinct and into insight. By using the tools and data available, organizations make faster, more accurate, and more consistent choices. It's not just about having reports—it's about building the habit of asking, "What does the data say?"

In the next part of this book, we shift our focus to **Data Literacy and Data Governance**, where we'll begin by exploring the **DIKW Framework** and how raw data transforms into meaningful knowledge and strategic wisdom.

Great, we're now starting **Part 6: Data Literacy and Data Governance**, which focuses on helping professionals not only understand data but also use it responsibly and accurately.

Let's begin with the first chapter in this section.

PART 6

DATA LITERACY AND DATA GOVERNANCE

Chapter 29
DIKW Framework: From Raw Data to Strategic Wisdom

In today's information-driven world, we are surrounded by data—but not all data leads to insight, and not all insight leads to action. To move from collecting data to making smart decisions, we need a structure that explains the transformation of data into value. That's where the **DIKW Framework** comes in: **Data, Information, Knowledge, Wisdom**.

This chapter introduces the DIKW pyramid and how it applies to business scenarios, helping professionals understand how raw numbers become meaningful action.

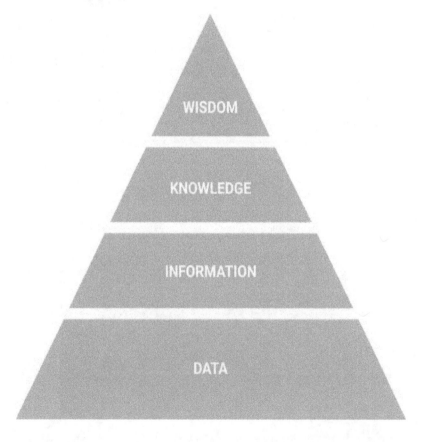

What Is the DIKW Framework?

The DIKW model describes the hierarchy of data processing and understanding:

1. **Data** – Raw, unorganized facts with no context.

2. **Information** – Data that has been processed and given meaning.

3. **Knowledge** – The application of information to a specific context.

4. **Wisdom** – Strategic judgment based on accumulated knowledge and experience.

Each layer builds on the one below it.

1. Data: The Raw Material

Data is the foundation. It can be numbers, symbols, or text collected from various sources like:

- Sales orders
- Attendance logs
- Customer surveys
- Sensor readings
- Social media interactions

On its own, data has no meaning. For example:

"28, 47, 55" — Without context, these are just numbers.

2. Information: Contextualized Data

When data is organized and placed in context, it becomes **information**. For example:

"28 orders on Monday, 47 on Tuesday, 55 on Wednesday."

Now the numbers are associated with days and events—making them useful.

Information answers basic questions like:

- Who?
- What?
- When?
- Where?

ERP and BI tools help transform data into usable information through reports, dashboards, and summaries.

3. Knowledge: Applied Information

Knowledge is about understanding relationships, patterns, and implications. It helps answer **"how"** something works.

For example:

- "Sales increased due to a promotional email sent Monday morning."
- "Inventory delays are linked to supplier X's change in shipping terms."

Knowledge enables decision-making. It may also be stored in SOPs, training materials, or employee experience.

4. Wisdom: Strategic Decision-Making

Wisdom is the ability to use knowledge with judgment. It answers the **"why"** and **"what should we do next?"**

For example:

- "We should launch all future promotions on Monday mornings for better impact."
- "We should diversify suppliers to reduce shipping delays."

Wisdom considers not just outcomes, but ethics, context, timing, and experience. It often resides in leadership, strategy teams, or consultants—but can be cultivated in any role.

Real-World Example: DIKW in Action

Let's say you work in customer service:

- **Data**: 50 calls received, 10 complaints logged, average call time = 6 minutes

- **Information**: Complaints increased by 20% on Monday morning

- **Knowledge**: Monday complaints are due to system slowness during weekend updates

- **Wisdom**: Reschedule updates to late Monday night, when call volume is lowest

Each step brings more clarity, insight, and strategic value.

Why DIKW Matters in the Workplace

- Helps employees understand the value of accurate data entry

- Encourages analysis, not just reporting

- Connects daily operations to bigger business goals

- Builds a culture of insight-driven improvement

Understanding this model helps professionals elevate from being data consumers to being insight contributors.

In Summary

The DIKW framework reminds us that data alone is not enough. True value comes from moving up the ladder—from raw facts to information, from understanding to action. Whether you're generating reports, making decisions, or solving problems, recognizing which level you're working at helps you ask better questions and deliver smarter solutions.

In the next chapter, we'll dive into **Data Collection, Validation, and Accuracy**—because good decisions begin with clean, trustworthy data.

Chapter 30
Data Collection, Validation, and Accuracy: Building a Foundation for Trustworthy Information

No matter how advanced your reporting tools or dashboards are, they are only as good as the data behind them. If data is entered incorrectly, collected inconsistently, or lacks validation, it leads to flawed insights, poor decisions, and even reputational damage. That's why every employee—regardless of role—must understand the basics of how data is collected, validated, and maintained accurately.

This chapter explores how data enters a business system, the importance of validating it at every step, and how to build a culture of accuracy across departments.

Understanding Data Collection in Business

Data enters business systems from a variety of sources. These can be:

- Manual entries by staff (e.g., sales orders, invoices, leave applications)

- Automated systems (e.g., sensors, scanners, APIs)

- Customer inputs (e.g., forms, support tickets, emails)

- Integrated apps (e.g., CRM, ERP, third-party platforms)

Each entry point introduces the risk of error—typos, duplicate entries, missing fields, or inconsistent formats.

For example, if a sales rep enters "Dubai" for location and another enters "DXB", reporting by region becomes inaccurate. Similarly, a missing product serial number may lead to issues in warranty tracking later.

Why Validation Matters

Validation ensures that data is complete, consistent, and correct before it's accepted by the system. It acts as a first line of defense against "bad data."

Common validation rules include:

- Required fields (e.g., customer name, email, amount)
- Format checks (e.g., email address must contain "@")
- Dropdown selections (e.g., only predefined departments or statuses)
- Duplicates detection (e.g., same invoice number entered twice)
- Cross-field checks (e.g., invoice date cannot be in the future)

Modern ERP systems often allow businesses to configure these rules and enforce them automatically.

Key Concepts: Clean vs. Dirty Data

- Clean Data: Complete, up to date, accurate, and consistent
- Dirty Data: Incomplete, outdated, inconsistent, or incorrect

Dirty data leads to:

- Reporting errors
- Missed opportunities
- Failed communications
- Operational delays

For example, incorrect contact details may mean that customers don't receive important notifications, while wrong inventory quantities can result in missed deliveries or stockouts.

Tips for Accurate Data Collection

1. Standardize Data Entry
2. Define naming conventions, field formats, and rules (e.g., all product names in uppercase, phone numbers in international format).

3. Use Drop-downs and Lookups

4. Whenever possible, avoid free-text fields. Dropdowns and linked master tables reduce variation and errors.

5. Enable Auto-Fill and Defaults

6. Pre-fill common fields where applicable to reduce manual entry and ensure consistency.

7. Train Staff

8. Data quality begins with awareness. Teach teams why accuracy matters and how to spot common entry errors.

9. Review and Clean Data Regularly

10. Set up periodic reviews to detect and correct outdated or invalid records. Use deduplication tools or scripts.

11. Use Validation Alerts

12. Let users know when they've missed a field or entered something incorrectly. Immediate feedback reduces mistakes.

13. Audit Trails

14. Enable tracking of who created or modified data and when. This promotes accountability and supports investigations.

Real-World Example

A company runs a marketing campaign using customer data from their CRM. Due to poor validation, 15% of email addresses are invalid, and several duplicate records result in customers receiving the same message twice. This leads to poor engagement and some unsubscribes. After cleaning the database, standardizing formats, and training sales staff on proper data entry, future campaigns see a 25% improvement in open rates and better targeting.

Impact of Bad Data on Reporting and Analytics

Imagine analyzing monthly revenue by customer segment, only to discover that some customers were tagged under different names ("ABC Ltd", "A B C Ltd.", "abc ltd"). This results in fragmented reports and incorrect conclusions. Ensuring accurate, validated data protects the integrity of all reports and decisions.

Your Role in Data Quality

You don't need to be a data analyst to improve data accuracy. Whether you're entering purchase requests, logging support tickets, updating employee records, or filling out forms, your attention to detail matters. Everyone contributes to the organization's data ecosystem.

In Summary

Accurate data is the foundation of trustworthy reporting, meaningful insights, and sound decision-making. By collecting data carefully, validating inputs, and reviewing records regularly, individuals and teams can reduce errors and improve operational performance. In the next chapter, we will learn how to read and interpret reports and dashboards—turning accurate data into actionable understanding.

Chapter 31
Reading and Interpreting Reports and Dashboards: Turning Numbers into Understanding

In every modern workplace, reports and dashboards are shared regularly—via emails, meetings, or internal portals. These might include a sales summary, an employee attendance report, a customer feedback dashboard, or a financial performance chart. But having access to data is not the same as understanding it.

This chapter is designed to help professionals of all levels read, interpret, and question reports and dashboards effectively, so they can make sense of the numbers and contribute meaningfully to decisions and discussions.

Why Report Interpretation Matters

Business reports and dashboards don't just serve analysts or executives. Every employee—from a junior accountant to a department manager—will be expected to review, understand, or act on data. Being able to:

- Read a chart correctly
- Spot trends or issues
- Ask the right questions
- Extract key messages

…is a skill that improves decision-making, productivity, and credibility.

Basic Elements of a Report

1. **Title and Time Frame**
2. Clearly state what the report is about and the period it covers (e.g., "Monthly Sales Report – March 2025").
3. **Filters and Criteria**

4. Know what's included or excluded. For example, is it showing all regions or just one? Are canceled orders excluded?

5. **Data Fields**

6. Understand what each column or metric means (e.g., "Gross Sales," "Net Profit," "Open Tickets," "Conversion Rate").

7. **Visualizations**

   o **Bar Charts**: Great for comparing categories

   o **Line Charts**: Show trends over time

   o **Pie Charts**: Show percentage distribution

   o **Tables**: Provide detailed breakdowns

   o **KPI Widgets**: Highlight critical metrics (e.g., today's revenue)

How to Read a Dashboard Effectively

1. **Start with High-Level KPIs**

2. These give a quick overview: sales growth, customer satisfaction, profit margin. Look for any values outside the normal range.

3. **Use Filters and Slicers**

4. Drill down by region, product, department, or time. This helps you find root causes or identify specific areas of concern.

5. **Look for Trends and Patterns**

6. Is performance improving, declining, or flat? Do results fluctuate at certain times of the day, week, or year?

7. **Compare Against Benchmarks**

8. Dashboards often include targets, past performance, or industry averages. Are we above or below expectations?

9. **Focus on Outliers and Exceptions**

10. A spike in expenses or a sudden drop in sales may reveal operational issues or opportunities that require immediate attention.

Examples of Interpretation in Practice

- **Sales Report**: "Sales are up 12% this month, but average order value has decreased—possibly due to more low-cost items being sold."

- **HR Dashboard**: "Attrition is highest among junior staff with under 6 months of tenure—indicating onboarding or culture gaps."

- **Customer Service Chart**: "Ticket resolution time has increased—despite lower ticket volume. This might indicate resource or process inefficiencies."

Tips for Interpreting Data Accurately

- Don't rely on one number—explore multiple indicators

- Ask "why" when you see a spike or drop

- Correlate different data points (e.g., high sales but also high return rate)

- Beware of seasonal effects, promotions, or one-time events

- Understand how the data is sourced and when it was last updated

Common Pitfalls to Avoid

- **Misreading scale or axis**: Always check if graphs use consistent intervals

- **Assuming correlation equals causation**: Just because two metrics rise together doesn't mean one causes the other

- **Ignoring anomalies**: Small unexpected changes may reveal larger underlying issues

- **Overlooking filters**: A report filtered to one region may not reflect the full picture

Becoming a Critical Data Consumer

You don't need to create dashboards to use them well. Ask:

- What is this report telling me?

- What's missing or unclear?

- What decision or action does this support?

- Is there another way to view the same data?

Critical thinking and curiosity are just as important as numbers on a screen.

In Summary

Reading and interpreting dashboards and reports is a key professional skill in the digital workplace. With practice, you'll not only be able to extract insights quickly but also challenge assumptions, spot trends early, and contribute meaningfully in meetings or reports. In the next chapter, we'll explore **Data Privacy Regulations**—so you understand what laws govern data use and how to handle it responsibly in your role.

Chapter 32
Data Privacy Regulations: Understanding Compliance and Responsibility in the Workplace

In a world where personal data is collected, stored, and shared at unprecedented levels, data privacy is no longer just a legal requirement—it's a business imperative. Whether you work in HR, marketing, IT, or customer service, handling data comes with responsibility. From collecting a customer's email address to processing payroll or using analytics tools, every action must comply with privacy laws.

This chapter introduces key data privacy regulations such as **GDPR** and local laws, explains why they matter, and shows how employees at all levels can stay compliant while respecting individuals' rights.

What Is Data Privacy?

Data privacy refers to the protection of individuals' personal information—ensuring that it is collected, used, stored, and shared in a lawful and ethical manner. Personal data can include:

- Full name, ID/passport number

- Email address and phone number

- Physical address

- IP address or location

- Financial information

- Employment and medical records

Any business that collects or processes personal data is obligated to protect it.

Key Global Data Privacy Regulations

1. GDPR (General Data Protection Regulation – Europe)

- Applies to any organization handling the data of EU citizens, regardless of the company's location

- Requires consent for data collection

- Grants individuals the right to access, correct, or delete their data

- Mandates breach notification within 72 hours

- Heavy fines for non-compliance (up to €20 million or 4% of annual revenue)

2. CCPA (California Consumer Privacy Act)

- Applies to companies doing business with California residents

- Gives consumers rights to access, delete, and opt out of data sales

- Requires businesses to disclose what personal data they collect and why

3. **Local Laws** (e.g., Oman, UAE, India, etc.)
   - Many countries have their own data protection laws
   - Typically cover consent, data usage, breach reporting, and transfer restrictions
   - Businesses must comply with local regulations in addition to any international laws if dealing with global clients

Key Principles of Data Privacy

- **Lawfulness, Fairness, and Transparency**: Individuals must be informed about how their data will be used
- **Purpose Limitation**: Data should only be collected for specific, legitimate purposes
- **Data Minimization**: Only necessary data should be collected
- **Accuracy**: Data should be kept up to date
- **Storage Limitation**: Personal data shouldn't be kept longer than needed
- **Integrity and Confidentiality**: Data must be protected from unauthorized access or loss

Common Workplace Scenarios

- **Marketing**: Cannot email users without their consent; must include unsubscribe options
- **HR**: Must protect employee files, limit access to sensitive information, and encrypt payroll data
- **Customer Service**: Cannot share a customer's data with another client or unrelated party
- **IT**: Must ensure secure storage, backup, and restricted access to sensitive data
- **Finance**: Must ensure financial records are accessible only to authorized personnel

Understanding Consent

Consent must be:

- **Freely given**: No pressure or coercion

- **Informed**: Clear explanation of what data will be used for

- **Specific**: Consent for one purpose doesn't mean consent for all

- **Revocable**: Users must be able to withdraw consent at any time

Example: A website that asks users to "tick a box" to receive marketing emails must also give them a way to unsubscribe later.

Data Breaches and Your Role

A data breach occurs when personal data is lost, stolen, exposed, or accessed without authorization. Causes include:

- Weak passwords

- Lost or stolen devices

- Phishing attacks

- Accidental sharing or printing of private documents

- Unsecured cloud storage

If you suspect a breach:

1. Report it immediately to your supervisor or IT/security team

2. Avoid deleting or tampering with data before reporting

3. Cooperate in the investigation

4. Learn from the incident and follow updated protocols

Best Practices for Employees

- Never share passwords or login credentials

- Lock your screen when away from your desk

- Use encrypted tools or secure platforms when handling personal data

- Verify requests before sending data—especially if the sender claims to be a manager or supplier

- Be cautious with spreadsheets or attachments containing personal data

- Attend mandatory data privacy training sessions

Real-World Example

An employee receives an email that appears to be from the CFO requesting customer payment information. Without verifying the email address, they send a spreadsheet with client banking details. This turns out to be a phishing scam, leading to a data breach and regulatory penalties. The incident could have been avoided with basic email verification and awareness of privacy protocols.

In Summary

Data privacy is not just the responsibility of the legal or IT departments—it is a shared duty across the organization. Understanding the laws, respecting individuals' rights, and applying safe practices helps build trust with customers and employees, reduces legal risks, and supports ethical business practices. In the next chapter, we'll explore **Ethical Use and Attribution of Data**, covering how to handle data responsibly and recognize its sources and ownership.

Chapter 33
Ethical Use and Attribution of Data: Responsibility, Ownership, and Respect in the Digital Age

Data is one of the most valuable assets in any organization. From customer behavior and market research to employee records and financials, businesses rely on data to operate, innovate, and grow. But with this power comes responsibility—not just legal, but ethical. How we collect, use, share, and give credit for data reflects our organizational values and integrity.

This chapter focuses on the **ethical principles** of using data in the workplace, the importance of proper **attribution**, and how professionals can uphold trust and fairness when working with information.

Why Ethics in Data Use Matters

While regulations like GDPR tell you what you **must** do, ethics guide what you **should** do—even when there's no law involved. Ethical data behavior builds:

- **Trust** with customers, employees, and partners
- **Reputation** as a responsible and transparent business
- **Internal culture** where honesty and accountability are valued

Poor data ethics can lead to legal trouble, employee dissatisfaction, customer backlash, or damage to your brand—even if no laws were technically broken.

Core Principles of Ethical Data Use

1. Transparency

People should know when and why their data is being collected. Surprise tracking or hidden monitoring violates this principle.

2. **Consent and Choice**

   Users must have the option to provide or withdraw data—especially personal or sensitive data.

3. **Minimization**

   Only collect what's necessary. Just because you can collect more data doesn't mean you should.

4. **Security**

   Ethical use includes protecting data from unauthorized access, leaks, or theft.

5. **Non-discrimination**

   Data should not be used to unfairly target, profile, or exclude individuals or groups.

6. **Purpose Limitation**

   Data collected for one purpose should not be reused for unrelated purposes without consent.

Real-World Examples of Ethical Misuse

- A marketing team uses job applicants' email addresses for promotional emails. Even if not illegal, it's unethical unless consent was given.

- A manager accesses an employee's medical leave records out of curiosity. Even if they have system access, it's a violation of privacy ethics.

- A business scrapes online content (like reviews or social media posts) for commercial use without credit or permission.

What Is Data Attribution?

Attribution means giving credit to the original source of the data. This is especially important when:

- Using third-party research, reports, or datasets
- Quoting statistics in presentations or proposals

- Sharing visualizations or charts created by others

Failing to attribute is a form of plagiarism. Just like in academic writing, business content must also respect intellectual property.

Examples of Proper Attribution

- "According to a 2024 report by McKinsey…"
- "Data sourced from Statista"
- In dashboards: "Source: Google Analytics, Jan–Mar 2025"
- Footnotes or watermarks on charts: "Internal Sales Data – ERP System"

Even when data is public or free, attribution helps maintain credibility and clarity.

Ethical Considerations for AI and Automation

As AI tools become more common, new ethical challenges arise:

- Is it clear when content was generated by AI (e.g., chatbots, reports)?
- Are AI tools trained on proprietary or personal data without consent?
- Are decisions being made by algorithms that users cannot question?

Ethical AI use involves human oversight, fairness, and clear boundaries.

Guidelines for Ethical Behavior with Data

- Always ask: "Would I be okay if my own data were used this way?"
- When in doubt, get consent—even if not legally required
- Verify data sources before using or sharing
- Avoid manipulating or misrepresenting data to suit a narrative
- Report misuse or unethical practices to your manager or compliance team

Role of Organizations

Organizations must set clear policies on:

- Data access rights

- Data usage guidelines

- Approval processes for sharing or publishing reports

- Whistleblower mechanisms for unethical behavior

In Summary

Ethical use of data is about more than compliance—it's about respect, responsibility, and professionalism. Whether you're handling customer data, using internal reports, or presenting insights from external sources, always consider the human and ethical implications. Doing the right thing—even when no one is watching—strengthens your credibility and the trust others place in your work.

In the next chapter, we begin **Part 7: Cybersecurity and Digital Safety**, where we'll learn how to protect systems, data, and individuals from the growing risks in the digital workplace.

PART 7

CYBERSECURITY AND DIGITAL SAFETY

Chapter 34
Cybersecurity Basics for All Roles: Everyone's Responsibility in the Digital Workplace

Cybersecurity is no longer just the concern of IT departments or cybersecurity experts. Every person in an organization—regardless of title or department—plays a role in protecting data, systems, and business operations. From clicking on an email link to connecting to public Wi-Fi, simple actions can open the door to major security breaches.

This chapter introduces the **core concepts of cybersecurity**, explains **common threats**, and highlights **essential habits** every employee should adopt to reduce risk in the digital workplace.

What Is Cybersecurity?

Cybersecurity is the practice of protecting systems, networks, and data from digital attacks. These attacks are designed to:

- Steal sensitive information (e.g., passwords, financial data)
- Disrupt business operations (e.g., ransomware attacks)
- Impersonate or deceive employees (e.g., phishing)
- Damage an organization's reputation

Cyber threats target everyone—from interns to CEOs—because human error is often the weakest link.

Why Cybersecurity Involves Everyone

- IT can set up firewalls and endpoint protection, but if a staff member clicks on a malicious email, the entire network may be compromised.
- Executives may be impersonated in fraudulent emails unless they verify messages properly.

- Customer service teams may accidentally expose client data through poor password practices.

Common Cyber Threats You Should Know

1. **Phishing**

   Fake emails or messages designed to trick users into revealing sensitive information or clicking malicious links.

2. **Malware**

   Harmful software like viruses, worms, or ransomware that can infect systems.

3. **Ransomware**

   Malware that locks access to files or systems until a ransom is paid.

4. **Social Engineering**

   Manipulating people into revealing confidential information through deception (e.g., pretending to be IT support or a vendor).

5. **Password Attacks**

   Hackers use software to guess or steal weak or reused passwords.

6. **Data Leaks**

   Accidental or intentional exposure of confidential data, often through email, file sharing, or lost devices.

Everyday Behaviors That Create Risk

- Clicking unknown links in emails
- Using the same password across multiple accounts
- Leaving devices unlocked or unattended
- Connecting to unsecured public Wi-Fi
- Forwarding work documents to personal email addresses
- Ignoring software updates and security patches

Core Cyber Hygiene Practices for Everyone

1. **Use Strong, Unique Passwords**

   Combine uppercase, lowercase, numbers, and symbols. Don't use "123456" or "password."

2. **Enable Multi-Factor Authentication (MFA)**

   MFA adds a second layer of protection—like a one-time code or biometric scan.

3. **Lock Your Devices**

   Always lock your screen when stepping away, even for a minute.

4. **Keep Software Updated**

   Install updates and patches for operating systems, browsers, and business apps promptly.

5. **Be Suspicious of Urgent Requests**

   If someone asks you to transfer funds, send sensitive data, or download a file urgently—verify by phone or in person.

6. **Don't Share Credentials**

   Never share your login details with colleagues, vendors, or external parties.

7. **Report Suspicious Activity**

   If you receive a suspicious email or see something unusual on your device, report it immediately to IT or security.

Real-World Example

An employee in the finance team receives an email that appears to be from the CEO, urgently requesting a wire transfer to a new vendor. The tone is demanding, and it's signed with the CEO's name. Without verifying, the employee processes the payment—only to find out later it was a spoofed email from a hacker. This type of **Business Email Compromise (BEC)** causes billions in global losses annually—and is preventable with awareness and verification.

Cybersecurity Isn't Just for the Office

With remote work, bring-your-own-device (BYOD) policies, and mobile access, employees must secure:

- Personal devices used for work
- Home Wi-Fi networks (with strong router passwords and encryption)
- Mobile phones (with screen locks, app permissions, and updated OS)

Your Role in Cybersecurity

- Follow your company's cybersecurity policies
- Participate in training and simulations
- Ask if unsure about a link, attachment, or request
- Don't take shortcuts with passwords or data sharing
- Stay alert—cybersecurity is part of your daily work routine

In Summary

Cybersecurity is not just an IT issue—it's a shared responsibility. Every employee has the power to protect or expose the organization to risk through their daily digital behavior. By understanding the basics, developing good habits, and staying cautious, you become an important line of defense against cyber threats.

In the next chapter, we'll explore **Malware, Ransomware, and Online Threats**, helping you recognize specific attack types and how to prevent them.

Master pfSense: Network Security & Firewall Management	

Chapter 35
Malware, Ransomware, and Online Threats: Recognizing and Preventing Digital Attacks

In the digital age, malicious software—or **malware**—has become one of the most common and dangerous threats to individuals and organizations. Whether it's a pop-up virus, a stealthy data stealer, or a system-crippling ransomware attack, these threats can cause massive financial, reputational, and operational damage.

This chapter breaks down what malware is, how it spreads, and what you can do—as a non-technical professional or a manager—to prevent, detect, and respond to such threats.

What Is Malware?

Malware (short for malicious software) refers to any program or file designed to infiltrate, damage, or disrupt systems without user consent. Malware can:

- Steal personal or business data
- Lock access to files or systems
- Monitor user activity
- Corrupt or delete files
- Spread across networks

Types of Malware and Online Threats

1. **Viruses**

   Malicious code that attaches itself to clean files and spreads from one system to another.

2. **Worms**

   Self-replicating programs that spread across networks without user action.

3. **Trojans**

Disguised as legitimate software. Once installed, they can give attackers control over the system.

4. **Ransomware**

Encrypts files or systems and demands payment for access. One of the most devastating forms of malware for businesses.

5. **Spyware**

Secretly records user actions—like keystrokes, screen activity, or browsing history—to collect sensitive data.

6. **Adware**

Bombards users with unwanted advertisements. Often bundled with free software.

7. **Rootkits**

Designed to hide malware deep in the system, making it difficult to detect or remove.

8. **Keyloggers**

Record every keystroke—commonly used to steal passwords, credit card numbers, or confidential text.

Ransomware: The Rising Threat

Ransomware has become a major business risk. Attackers may:

- Lock all files on a computer or entire network
- Demand payment in cryptocurrency (Bitcoin)
- Threaten to leak confidential data if payment isn't made

Even paying the ransom doesn't guarantee recovery, and it encourages further attacks.

How Malware Gets In

- Clicking on links in phishing emails
- Downloading attachments from unknown sources

- Visiting fake or infected websites

- Installing software from unofficial sites

- Using infected USB drives

- Weak or outdated antivirus protection

Real-World Example

In a mid-sized company, a staff member downloads what appears to be an invoice attachment. It installs ransomware that spreads across the network, locking the company's accounting files. The company cannot send invoices or access historical data. A ransom of $25,000 in Bitcoin is demanded. Despite recovery efforts, it takes two weeks to restore operations—and costs over $80,000 in downtime and recovery services.

Warning Signs of a Malware Infection

- Unusual system slowdown

- Frequent crashes or pop-ups

- Unauthorized changes in settings

- Files missing, renamed, or encrypted

- Unexpected network activity

- Fake antivirus warnings or system messages

Preventive Measures for Everyone

1. **Don't click suspicious links or open unknown attachments**

   If in doubt, verify with the sender.

2. **Install and update antivirus/antimalware software**

   Ensure real-time protection is enabled and run full scans regularly.

3. **Update your operating system and software**

   Many attacks exploit outdated software with known vulnerabilities.

4. **Use secure web browsers and avoid untrusted websites**

   Enable pop-up blockers and consider browser extensions that block trackers and threats.

5. **Never plug in unknown USB drives**

Malware can spread through infected external devices.

6. **Back up data regularly**

Use secure cloud backups or offline storage. This is crucial in case of ransomware.

7. **Report suspicious activity immediately**

 If you think your system has been infected, disconnect from the network and inform IT.

Role of Organizations in Malware Protection

- Implement endpoint protection and email filtering
- Block access to known malicious websites
- Conduct employee awareness training
- Regularly test systems with simulated attacks (penetration testing)
- Maintain data backups and recovery plans

Your Role

Even if you're not in IT, you have a role to play:

- Be cautious, especially with emails and downloads
- Report anything strange—better safe than sorry
- Follow your company's cybersecurity policy
- Support others by promoting awareness

In Summary

Malware and ransomware are evolving constantly—but the majority of attacks succeed because of human error. With basic awareness and good digital habits, you can protect your devices, your organization, and your personal data from becoming a victim. In the next chapter, we'll explore **Phishing, Impersonation, and Social Engineering**, diving deeper into the psychological tactics attackers use to manipulate people into giving up access.

Chapter 36
Phishing, Impersonation, and Social Engineering: Outsmarting the Human Hack

While many cyber threats are technical, the most common and dangerous attacks target people—not systems. These attacks rely on **manipulation, trust, and urgency** to trick individuals into revealing information, clicking malicious links, or sending money. This type of attack is known as **social engineering**.

This chapter covers phishing, impersonation, and social engineering in the workplace. You'll learn how attackers exploit human behavior, how to recognize warning signs, and what steps to take to avoid falling victim.

What Is Social Engineering?

Social engineering is the act of deceiving people into giving away confidential information or access, usually by pretending to be someone trustworthy. Instead of hacking software, social engineers "hack" human psychology.

Social engineering works because:

- People are helpful by nature
- Most employees don't question authority
- Urgency pressures people into acting fast
- Curiosity or fear override caution

Phishing: The Most Common Attack

Phishing is when attackers send emails that look real—but are actually fake. They often pretend to be:

- Your boss or CEO

- Your bank or a government agency

- A trusted vendor or client

- IT support or HR

The goal is to get you to:

- Click on a malicious link

- Download malware

- Enter your password or financial info

- Send sensitive documents
- Transfer money to a fake account

Types of Phishing

1. **Email Phishing**: Generic, wide-scale attacks pretending to be from known companies (e.g., "Your Microsoft account has been locked").

2. **Spear Phishing**: Highly targeted, personalized emails using names, job titles, or company info to increase trust.

3. **Whaling**: Targeting executives with fake invoices, legal threats, or urgent fund transfer requests.

4. **Smishing**: Phishing via SMS or messaging apps ("Click here to confirm your delivery").

5. **Vishing**: Voice phishing over the phone. Attackers may impersonate banks, support staff, or government agents.

Impersonation in Action

Attackers may:

- Use a fake email address that looks nearly identical to a real one (e.g., ceo@yourcomapny.com instead of ceo@yourcompany.com)
- Copy email signatures, logos, and language styles
- Use real names or titles found on LinkedIn
- Reply to existing email chains to seem legitimate

Real-World Example

An employee receives an email that appears to be from the head of procurement, asking them to urgently pay a supplier due to a system error. The email includes the correct name, job title, and even a chain of prior emails (spoofed). Without verifying, the employee transfers $15,000 to an international account. Later, it's discovered that the supplier's real email account had been hacked weeks earlier.

Psychological Tactics Used by Social Engineers

- **Authority**: "This is from your CEO—do it now."
- **Urgency**: "We need this resolved immediately!"
- **Fear**: "Your account will be suspended."
- **Curiosity**: "Unusual login detected—check here."
- **Helpfulness**: "Can you reset my password quickly?"
- **Greed**: "You've won a gift card!"

How to Spot Phishing or Impersonation

- The email address is slightly off
- Unusual tone or urgency that doesn't match the person's normal style
- Poor spelling or grammar
- Unexpected attachments or links
- Requests for money, gift cards, passwords, or sensitive data
- Domain name doesn't match the sender (e.g., using Gmail for company communication)

What You Should Do

1. **Pause** – Don't act on emotion or pressure.
2. **Verify** – Call or message the person through known channels.
3. **Check email details** – Hover over links, examine sender addresses.
4. **Report** – Use your company's phishing report option or contact IT/security.
5. **Never reply to suspicious messages** – It confirms your account is active.

Best Practices to Prevent Social Engineering Attacks

- Be skeptical of unsolicited messages—especially ones asking for credentials or money.

- Don't use links from emails to log in—go to the official website manually.

- Use multifactor authentication—so stolen passwords alone aren't enough.

- Don't post sensitive job details publicly (e.g., "I approve payments for XYZ Corp").

- Educate your team with phishing simulations and awareness sessions.

- Encourage a no-blame culture for reporting near misses or mistakes.

Social Engineering via AI: The New Threat

With deepfake videos and AI-generated voice or text, attackers now impersonate people more convincingly than ever:

- A fake video of the CEO announcing a payment

- A phone call that sounds like your manager

- A chatbot posing as support on a fake website

Always verify through known, secure methods—especially if money or sensitive data is involved.

In Summary

Social engineering doesn't exploit software—it exploits human trust. It can happen to anyone, regardless of experience or role. By understanding how these attacks work, staying alert to red flags, and promoting a culture of verification and reporting, every employee becomes a line of defense.

In the next chapter, we'll cover **Common Mistakes and How to Avoid Them**, showing how simple habits can make a huge difference in protecting personal and company data.

Chapter 37
Common Mistakes and How to Avoid Them: Strengthening Everyday Cyber Habits

Cybersecurity is not just about firewalls and antivirus software—it's also about people. Most cyber incidents are not caused by hackers exploiting software vulnerabilities, but by human errors: weak passwords, clicking unsafe links, or sharing data carelessly. These are simple mistakes, yet they can lead to major breaches.

In this chapter, we will examine the **most common cybersecurity mistakes employees make**, explain why they happen, and offer practical ways to avoid them—regardless of your role or technical background.

Mistake 1: Using Weak or Reused Passwords

One of the easiest ways attackers gain access to systems is by cracking weak passwords—or using credentials leaked from previous breaches. Using the same password across work and personal accounts multiplies the risk.

What to Do Instead

- Use long, complex passwords (mix of letters, numbers, symbols)
- Never reuse passwords between services
- Use a password manager to generate and store strong, unique passwords
- Enable Multi-Factor Authentication (MFA) wherever possible

Mistake 2: Clicking on Suspicious Links or Attachments

Phishing emails often look legitimate and may create a sense of urgency. One careless click can lead to malware installation or account compromise.

What to Do Instead

- Check the sender's email address carefully

- Hover over links to see where they lead

- Don't open attachments from unknown or unexpected sources

- When in doubt, verify with the sender through a different channel

Mistake 3: Ignoring Software Updates

Many people delay or ignore update notifications—assuming they're optional. But software updates often include patches for known vulnerabilities that attackers actively exploit.

What to Do Instead

- Turn on automatic updates for your operating system, browser, and business apps

- Regularly check for updates if auto-update is not available

- Restart your device when prompted after installing updates

Mistake 4: Leaving Devices Unlocked or Unattended

Walking away from a computer without locking the screen, or leaving a phone on a desk, allows anyone nearby to access sensitive information or send messages from your account.

What to Do Instead

- Lock your screen before leaving your desk (e.g., Windows + L, or closing your laptop lid)

- Set devices to auto-lock after a short period of inactivity

- Never leave laptops, phones, or USB drives in public or shared spaces unattended

Mistake 5: Sharing Confidential Information Carelessly

Sharing passwords with coworkers, sending documents to personal email accounts, or uploading files to unapproved cloud storage are all risky practices.

What to Do Instead

- Only share information with authorized people, through approved channels

- Avoid sending work data to personal accounts or devices

- Use your company's secure file-sharing or collaboration tools

Mistake 6: Not Reporting Suspicious Activity

Some employees hesitate to report strange emails or unexpected system behavior—either because they think it's nothing, or they fear getting blamed.

What to Do Instead

- Report suspicious activity immediately to IT or the security team

- Don't try to "fix" it yourself—disconnect from the network if necessary and wait for instructions

- Encourage a no-blame culture so people feel safe reporting issues

Mistake 7: Trusting Unknown Devices and Networks

Plugging in a USB drive of unknown origin or connecting to unsecured public Wi-Fi can open up your device to malware or monitoring.

What to Do Instead

- Never use unknown USBs or external drives

- Avoid accessing company data over public Wi-Fi without a VPN

- Use mobile hotspots or secured networks when working remotely

Mistake 8: Oversharing on Social Media or Public Platforms

Cybercriminals collect personal and professional details from social profiles to craft convincing phishing attacks or impersonations.

What to Do Instead

- Avoid sharing job details like "I manage payments for ABC Ltd."
- Don't reveal travel plans, internal systems, or email addresses publicly
- Adjust privacy settings on your social media accounts

Mistake 9: Assuming Cybersecurity Is Someone Else's Job

Employees often believe cybersecurity is solely the responsibility of the IT department, but everyone interacts with systems and data daily.

What to Do Instead

- Understand that security is a shared responsibility
- Follow policies and best practices, even for small tasks
- Stay informed through training sessions and company updates

Mistake 10: Using Personal Devices for Work Without Safeguards

With remote work and BYOD (Bring Your Own Device), using personal laptops or phones can introduce vulnerabilities if not secured properly.

What to Do Instead

- Use company-approved security tools (antivirus, VPN, mobile device management)
- Keep personal and work data separate
- Inform IT if you're using a personal device for work purposes

In Summary

Most security breaches start with small, preventable mistakes. By building good habits—strong passwords, cautious clicking, timely updates, and proper reporting—you reduce risk for yourself and your organization. Cybersecurity is not about being perfect, but about being aware, alert, and proactive.

In the next chapter, we'll explore **Cyber Hygiene Essentials** such as password managers, MFA, secure browsing, and device maintenance—turning awareness into action.

Chapter 38
Cyber Hygiene Essentials: Practical Habits for Everyday Digital Safety

Just like personal hygiene keeps you physically healthy, **cyber hygiene** refers to the regular practices and behaviors that keep your digital environment secure. These simple, ongoing actions reduce your vulnerability to threats like malware, phishing, unauthorized access, and data leaks.

This chapter focuses on practical, easy-to-follow habits that professionals can adopt—regardless of technical background—to stay protected in daily work and personal computing.

What Is Cyber Hygiene?

Cyber hygiene is the routine maintenance of your digital life: using secure passwords, updating software, backing up data, and being mindful of how you use devices and networks. The goal is to minimize risk and build resilience against cyber threats.

Good cyber hygiene makes you:

- Less likely to fall victim to scams or malware

- More aware of suspicious behaviors or phishing attempts

- More prepared to recover in case of a cyber incident

Core Cyber Hygiene Practices

1. Use a Password Manager

Creating and remembering unique, complex passwords for every account is nearly impossible without help. A password manager:

- Generates strong, random passwords

- Stores them securely in an encrypted vault

- Auto-fills credentials only on the correct websites

Popular options include LastPass, 1Password, Bitwarden, and browser-integrated managers like Google Password Manager or Microsoft Edge's built-in vault.

2. Enable Multi-Factor Authentication (MFA)

MFA adds a second layer of verification—typically a code sent to your phone or app—so even if your password is stolen, attackers can't log in.

Use MFA for:

- Email

- Cloud storage (Google Drive, OneDrive)

- Bank and financial accounts

- Remote access tools (VPNs, dashboards)

- Social media and online services

3. Keep Software and Devices Updated

Outdated apps, operating systems, and browser plugins are prime targets for cybercriminals.

Good habits:

- Turn on automatic updates
- Restart your computer regularly to apply updates
- Don't ignore update prompts on phones and apps
- Uninstall unused software

4. Secure Your Web Browsing

Your browser is a common entry point for threats. Protect it by:

- Installing a reputable ad-blocker
- Using HTTPS websites only (look for the padlock in the address bar)
- Avoiding suspicious pop-ups or download prompts
- Clearing cache and cookies regularly
- Using a privacy-conscious browser like Firefox or Brave, if preferred

5. Regularly Back Up Your Data

Backups protect you from data loss due to ransomware, hardware failure, or accidental deletion.

Best practices:

- Use both cloud and offline (external drive) backups
- Automate backups where possible
- Ensure backups are encrypted and stored securely
- Test recovery periodically to confirm they work

6. Lock and Secure Your Devices

Physical access is a common weak point in cybersecurity.

Do the following:

172

- Use strong device passwords or biometric login (face/fingerprint)
- Lock screens when stepping away
- Configure auto-lock timers
- Don't leave laptops, phones, or USB drives unattended in public

7. **Practice Safe File Handling**

Files—especially from unknown sources—can carry malware or sensitive information.

Be cautious about:

- Opening attachments without verifying the sender
- Downloading files from unofficial sources
- Uploading confidential files to unapproved cloud apps
- Forwarding sensitive documents without encryption or clearance

8. **Be Smart About App Permissions**

Many mobile and desktop apps ask for permissions they don't need.

Tips:

- Review and limit app permissions (e.g., location, microphone, camera)
- Only download apps from trusted stores (Google Play, Apple App Store)
- Remove apps you no longer use

9. **Be Mindful of Public Wi-Fi**

Public Wi-Fi networks are often unsecured and easy to exploit.

To protect yourself:

- Use a VPN (Virtual Private Network) when connecting to public networks
- Avoid logging into sensitive accounts (banking, work email)
- Disable file sharing and auto-connect options on your device
- Use mobile data when possible

10. **Audit Your Digital Footprint**

Know what data is out there about you, and take control where possible.

How:

- Google yourself periodically

- Remove unused online accounts

- Be selective about what you share on social media

- Avoid using work credentials to sign up for external services

Real-World Example

An employee loses a company-issued phone at the airport. Thanks to good cyber hygiene:

- The device was protected with biometric lock and PIN

- Sensitive apps were secured with MFA

- The device was enrolled in mobile device management (MDM), allowing IT to remotely wipe it

This incident, while inconvenient, did not lead to a data breach or compliance issue.

In Summary

Cyber hygiene isn't about being paranoid—it's about being prepared. These habits aren't technical or time-consuming, but they are essential. Practicing them regularly helps you avoid mistakes, protect company and personal data, and contribute to a safer digital environment for everyone.

In the next chapter, we'll discuss **Safe Internet and Cloud Usage**, focusing on best practices when browsing online, using cloud tools, and storing information across platforms.

Chapter 39
Safe Internet and Cloud Usage: Navigating the Digital World Responsibly

In the modern workplace, nearly every activity—from checking email and managing projects to accessing ERP systems and sharing files—happens over the internet or cloud platforms. While these tools offer convenience and scalability, they also introduce risks if not used carefully.

This chapter will help you understand how to browse the internet safely, use cloud services responsibly, and avoid common pitfalls that could compromise personal or organizational security.

Understanding the Risks of the Online World

Many cyberattacks begin with innocent internet use. Visiting untrusted websites, clicking pop-up ads, or using free cloud storage services without safeguards can open doors to:

- Malware infections
- Phishing scams
- Credential theft
- Data leaks
- Unauthorized access to sensitive files

Even trusted websites can be compromised. That's why awareness and discipline in your online behavior are crucial.

Safe Internet Browsing Practices

1. Use Secure Connections (HTTPS)

Always ensure the website you're visiting uses HTTPS, especially when entering login or payment information. Look for the padlock icon in your browser address bar.

2. **Avoid Public Wi-Fi for Sensitive Work**

Never log in to business systems or conduct financial transactions over unsecured public Wi-Fi. If you must use public Wi-Fi, connect through a VPN.

3. **Be Cautious with Downloads and Extensions**

Only download files, browser extensions, or software from trusted sources. Fake extensions can spy on you or steal data.

4. **Don't Click on Pop-Ups or Ads**

Even harmless-looking ads or alerts like "Your system is infected!" can lead to malicious sites or downloads.

5. **Use a Privacy-Focused Browser or Plugins**

Consider browsers or extensions that block ads, trackers, and malicious scripts (e.g., uBlock Origin, DuckDuckGo Privacy Essentials).

6. **Log Out When Finished**

Especially on shared or public devices, always log out from websites and close the browser window when done.

Using Cloud Services Safely

Cloud services like Google Drive, Microsoft OneDrive, Dropbox, and iCloud allow us to store and access files from anywhere. But cloud use must be managed securely.

1. **Use Company-Approved Platforms**

Always use the cloud platforms officially adopted by your organization. Avoid uploading company files to personal accounts or unknown storage tools.

2. **Enable Two-Factor Authentication (2FA)**

Cloud accounts often contain sensitive documents—adding a second layer of authentication helps prevent unauthorized access.

3. **Check Sharing Permissions**

Before sharing files or folders:

- Avoid "Anyone with the link can view" unless necessary

- Use "View Only" instead of "Edit" when possible

- Remove access when no longer needed

4. **Avoid Uploading Sensitive Information Without Encryption**

If a document includes financial data, personal IDs, or confidential strategies, consider encrypting it before storing in the cloud.

5. **Monitor Activity Logs (if available)**

Many cloud services allow you to see who accessed or downloaded a file. Use this feature to detect unusual behavior.

6. **Backup Your Cloud Data**

Cloud platforms can experience outages or account issues. Maintain local backups of critical files.

Real-World Example

An employee shares a Google Drive link with an external supplier but forgets to set permissions. The document includes internal pricing and customer contact details. Since it was set to "Anyone with the link," it got indexed by a search engine and became publicly accessible. The issue wasn't discovered until a competitor accessed it.

This mistake could have been prevented by reviewing sharing settings before sending the link.

Tips for Safe Cloud Collaboration

- Label documents clearly so users know what's sensitive

- Review access settings regularly, especially on shared folders

- Keep your cloud storage organized—cluttered drives increase the chance of sharing the wrong file

- Use watermarking or file expiration dates for temporary sharing

Your Role in Keeping Cloud and Internet Use Secure

- Be mindful of what you're clicking, downloading, or sharing

- Always question whether you're using the most secure method to access or send data

- Avoid mixing personal and business files on the same cloud drive

- If unsure, ask your IT or security team before using a new cloud tool or website

In Summary

Safe internet and cloud usage isn't about limiting productivity—it's about working smart and staying secure. By adopting cautious habits, using approved platforms, and applying thoughtful sharing practices, you protect not only yourself but your entire organization. In the next chapter, we'll explore **Device Management and BYOD (Bring Your Own Device) Policies**, which cover how to secure the phones, laptops, and personal devices that connect to your company's network.

Chapter 40
Device Management and BYOD Policies: Securing Laptops, Phones, and Personal Devices at Work

As the workplace becomes increasingly mobile and flexible, many employees use laptops, tablets, or smartphones—sometimes their own—for work purposes. This shift brings productivity benefits but also introduces new risks. Unmanaged or insecure devices can serve as gateways for malware, data leaks, or unauthorized access to corporate systems.

This chapter explains how organizations manage devices, what employees need to know about BYOD (Bring Your Own Device) policies, and how to keep both personal and work devices secure.

Why Device Management Matters

Every device connected to your company's network—whether it's a company-issued laptop or a personal smartphone—can be exploited if not properly secured. For example:

- An outdated app on a phone may be vulnerable to hacking

- A lost tablet could expose sensitive customer data

- An employee logging in from an infected home computer could spread malware to the business network

That's why IT departments implement device management tools and policies to monitor, secure, and support devices.

What Is Device Management?

Device management refers to the use of software and policies to control how devices access company systems. It allows IT to:

- Enforce encryption and password rules

- Remotely wipe data from lost or stolen devices

- Install or block apps

- Monitor compliance with security policies

- Push security updates and patches

Common tools include Microsoft Intune, Jamf, VMware Workspace ONE, and MobileIron.

Understanding BYOD: Bring Your Own Device

BYOD allows employees to use personal devices (phones, tablets, or laptops) for work activities—like accessing email, using collaboration tools, or logging into company portals. While convenient, BYOD comes with challenges.

Risks of BYOD include:

- Mixing personal and corporate data

- Lack of control over device security

- Use of unsecured apps or networks

- Potential for data leaks if devices are lost or stolen

What Employees Need to Know About BYOD Policies

1. Use only approved apps and platforms for work

2. Agree to basic security controls (e.g., screen lock, encryption, remote wipe)

3. Keep work and personal data separate when possible

4. Don't allow others (friends, family) to access your work apps

5. Notify IT immediately if your device is lost, stolen, or compromised

6. Accept that IT may need to monitor or restrict certain features on BYOD devices

Best Practices for Securing All Devices

Use a passcode or biometric lock

Avoid using simple PINs like 1234 or easily guessable passwords

Keep your operating system and apps updated

Install patches and updates regularly to fix known vulnerabilities

Enable automatic locking and short idle timeouts

This helps protect data if the device is left unattended

Install antivirus and mobile security apps

Even smartphones can be infected—especially through malicious apps

Encrypt sensitive data

Many devices support full-disk encryption or encrypted containers for corporate apps

Avoid jailbreaking or rooting

This weakens the device's built-in security protections and increases risk

Use VPNs when working remotely

A Virtual Private Network encrypts your internet traffic and protects it from spying on public networks

Avoid using public USB charging stations

Attackers can use these to install malware. Use your own charger and wall socket

Be careful with Bluetooth and file-sharing features

Disable them when not needed to prevent unauthorized access

Real-World Example

An employee uses their personal phone to check work email and download attachments. The phone doesn't have a screen lock or antivirus, and one day it's lost in a taxi. Since the email app was still open, anyone could access client correspondence and internal reports. Because the phone wasn't enrolled in mobile device management, IT couldn't remotely wipe it. The company faced reputational damage and had to report the incident under local data protection laws.

Creating a Culture of Shared Responsibility

Whether you use company-owned equipment or your own device, you're responsible for keeping it secure. Think of your device as a doorway to the organization's network—if it's left open, the entire business is at risk.

Always follow the company's device and BYOD policy, attend security awareness sessions, and ask IT if you have questions about using your devices safely for work.

In Summary

Device security is not just about the hardware—it's about how we use it. With the rise of BYOD, hybrid work, and mobile apps, employees must take a proactive role in protecting the devices they rely on. By following best practices and respecting device management policies, you help build a secure, productive digital workplace. In the next chapter, we'll cover Physical Security in the Office, focusing on how to protect systems and data in the physical environment—not just the digital one.

Chapter 41
Physical Security in the Office: Protecting Systems, Devices, and Data in the Real World

When people think of cybersecurity, they often focus on firewalls, passwords, and encryption. But many security breaches happen not through hacking—but through **physical access**. A lost laptop, an unlocked server room, or a visitor wandering into a restricted area can pose just as much risk as a phishing email.

This chapter focuses on **physical security measures** that all employees should understand and follow to protect their workplace environment, equipment, and sensitive information.

Why Physical Security Matters

Technology alone can't protect an organization if the physical access points—like office doors, desks, and devices—aren't secured. For example:

- A thief stealing a company laptop can access stored files if the device isn't encrypted

- An unattended screen could allow a passerby to read sensitive emails

- A tailgating visitor might access restricted departments without a badge

Physical and digital security go hand in hand. One weak link can break the entire chain.

Core Principles of Physical Security

1. Access Control

Only authorized individuals should be allowed to enter secure areas. This is typically managed through ID cards, biometric scanners, or digital access logs.

2. **Surveillance and Monitoring**

Offices often use CCTV cameras to deter theft and investigate incidents. But cameras aren't useful unless they're actively monitored and well-placed.

3. **Device Protection**

Desktops, laptops, projectors, and other devices should be locked, anchored, or kept in secure areas—especially after hours or during travel.

4. **Clean Desk Policy**

Employees should avoid leaving confidential documents, printouts, or USB drives unattended. Sensitive paperwork should be locked away when not in use.

5. **Screen Locking and Privacy**

6. Devices should auto-lock when idle. Screen privacy filters can also prevent shoulder surfing in open workspaces.

Employee Responsibilities

- **Always wear your ID badge** and challenge unfamiliar individuals without visible credentials

- **Don't allow tailgating**, where someone follows you through a secure door without scanning their own badge

- **Lock your screen** when leaving your desk, even for a short break

- **Store laptops and devices** in locked drawers or cabinets when not in use

- **Dispose of documents properly** using shredders or secure disposal bins—don't throw sensitive material in open trash

- **Report suspicious activity** or individuals loitering in restricted areas

Protecting Physical Data Assets

While much of today's data is digital, some records still exist in physical form—contracts, invoices, HR files, or customer applications. These too require protection:

- Lock filing cabinets and rooms where sensitive data is stored
- Limit access to documents to only those who need it
- Avoid printing sensitive data unless necessary

Securing Server Rooms and Network Equipment

Your office may have servers, switches, or network storage devices. These must be physically protected.

- Server rooms should be locked and accessible only to IT staff
- Equipment racks should be caged and bolted to the floor
- Unauthorized portable devices (like USBs or external hard drives) should be restricted from use in these areas

Visitors and Contractors

Visitors should:

- Be registered and given visitor badges
- Be accompanied at all times in restricted areas
- Not be allowed to use unattended workstations
- Not be permitted to plug in devices without IT approval

Remote Work and Physical Security

Even when working from home or in a co-working space, physical security still applies:

- Don't leave your laptop or phone in a car or public space unattended
- Use screen filters in shared environments (cafés, lounges, airports)
- Avoid working near strangers when discussing or displaying sensitive company material

Real-World Example

A staff member left a printed salary report on a shared printer in a common area. Another employee picked it up by mistake and shared the contents without realizing the sensitivity. Though unintentional, this breach led to internal conflict, HR complaints, and the need for a formal review of printing practices.

In Summary

Cybersecurity starts with people and places. By maintaining physical discipline—like locking screens, securing rooms, and managing access—you help prevent unauthorized use, theft, and breaches. Good physical security builds trust, protects assets, and supports your organization's overall information security posture.

In the next chapter, we'll focus on **Remote Work Security Practices**, addressing how to stay protected while working outside of traditional office environments.

Chapter 42
Remote Work Security Practices: Staying Safe Beyond the Office Walls

Remote work—whether from home, a café, or while traveling—offers flexibility, convenience, and productivity. But it also introduces unique security risks. Without the physical protections and controlled networks of a traditional office, employees working remotely become prime targets for cyber threats, data leaks, and device theft.

This chapter explains how to stay secure when working remotely, covering best practices for home setups, public spaces, and remote access tools.

Why Remote Work Increases Risk

When you work remotely, you rely on:

- Home Wi-Fi or public internet connections

- Personal or shared devices

- Uncontrolled physical environments

- Your own habits for locking devices, managing files, and ensuring privacy

This makes remote workers a preferred entry point for attackers looking to breach company networks.

Key Threats in Remote Work Settings

1. Unsecured Wi-Fi Networks

Home routers may be misconfigured or outdated. Public networks may be monitored by attackers.

2. Device Theft or Loss

Laptops or phones left unattended in cafés, airports, or cars can be stolen or accessed.

3. **Phishing and Social Engineering**

Remote workers may receive urgent-looking emails and have less direct support to verify them.

4. **Mixing Personal and Work Data**

Using the same device for personal browsing, email, and entertainment increases risk of malware and data leakage.

5. **Lack of Physical Privacy**

Working in public spaces exposes screens and conversations to onlookers.

Best Practices for Remote Work Security

1. Secure Your Home Network

- Change your default Wi-Fi router password and use strong WPA2/WPA3 encryption
- Keep your router firmware updated
- Disable remote access unless needed
- Avoid sharing your home Wi-Fi with untrusted guests

2. Use a VPN (Virtual Private Network)

A VPN encrypts your internet traffic and protects it from being monitored—especially important on public networks.

- Always connect to the company VPN before accessing internal systems
- Use company-approved VPN software
- Disconnect from VPN when not needed to reduce exposure

3. Keep Devices Updated and Secured

- Enable full-disk encryption
- Use biometric or strong password login
- Turn on auto-lock and screen timeout

- Install antivirus or endpoint protection tools provided by your organization
- Don't use outdated personal devices for work if they lack updates or security features

4. Be Mindful in Public Spaces

- Use a screen privacy filter when working in cafés or airports
- Avoid discussing sensitive topics in public
- Keep devices with you at all times—don't leave them on tables unattended
- Use headphones for meetings to protect confidential conversations

5. Separate Work and Personal Usage

- Don't install personal software or games on work devices
- Avoid accessing social media or unrelated websites on work equipment
- Use separate browsers or user profiles for work and personal activities
- Store work files only in company-authorized cloud platforms—not on USBs or personal drives

6. Use Strong Authentication Methods

- Always use multi-factor authentication for cloud platforms, email, and ERP systems
- Avoid saving passwords in browsers without a secure password manager
- Report unusual login alerts immediately

7. Follow Data Handling Policies

- Don't download sensitive documents to local storage unless necessary
- Don't print sensitive files at home unless secured

- Delete files that are no longer needed, and clear downloads regularly

- Avoid sending work files through personal email or messaging apps

8. Report Incidents Immediately

If your device is lost, stolen, or compromised, notify your IT/security team without delay—even if you're unsure of the impact. Time is critical in preventing further damage.

Real-World Example

A marketing manager working from a coworking space left their laptop on the table during a lunch break. In 10 minutes, it was gone. The laptop contained unreleased campaign files and client contracts. Although it had a password, it lacked encryption and VPN was left connected. The organization had to notify clients of potential data exposure and implement stricter remote work policies.

Creating a Remote Work Culture of Security

Security must be part of remote work culture—not an afterthought. Organizations can support this by:

- Providing secure devices and accessories

- Offering regular security training tailored to remote work

- Making reporting channels accessible and judgment-free

- Encouraging teams to share tips and solutions for secure remote practices

In Summary

Remote work doesn't have to mean compromised security. With the right habits, tools, and awareness, you can protect your work environment wherever you go. By securing devices, using VPNs, following data handling protocols, and staying vigilant, you become a strong link in your organization's remote security chain.

In the next chapter, we'll explore **Deepfakes, Voice Spoofing, and AI Threats**, examining how advanced technologies can deceive even the most alert professionals—and how to spot them.

Chapter 43
Deepfakes, Voice Spoofing, and AI Threats: Navigating the Next Generation of Digital Deception

As artificial intelligence (AI) technology advances, cybercriminals are using it not only to automate attacks but also to create highly convincing fake content. What used to be science fiction—imitating someone's face, voice, or writing style—is now a reality. These threats are harder to detect and can bypass traditional security tools by targeting human trust.

This chapter explores **deepfakes**, **voice spoofing**, and **AI-generated attacks**, and how employees and organizations can recognize, question, and defend against this emerging category of social engineering.

What Are Deepfakes and Voice Spoofing?

- **Deepfakes**: AI-generated videos or images where someone's face or body is manipulated to say or do things they never actually did.

- **Voice Spoofing**: AI-generated audio that mimics a person's voice, often used in phone calls or voicemails to trick victims.

- **AI-Generated Text**: Emails, messages, or chat conversations written by AI models that mimic a person's tone or language.

These tools can be used in fraud, extortion, impersonation, and misinformation campaigns—and they are getting more realistic by the day.

How These Threats Work in Real-World Scenarios

1. **Fake CEO Video**: A deepfake video shows the CEO asking all department heads to urgently wire funds to a new vendor. The message looks authentic, complete with corporate background and signature style.

2. **Voice-Based Fraud Call**: A finance staff member receives a phone call with what sounds like the CFO's voice authorizing a

confidential payment. The voice includes familiar mannerisms and speech patterns.

3. **AI-Written Email**: An employee receives a detailed and well-written email "from HR" requesting sensitive documents. The email tone matches previous HR communications and includes internal terminology—because it was trained on leaked internal documents.

4. **Social Media Manipulation**: A fake video of an executive making controversial statements goes viral, damaging the company's public image.

These attacks don't just rely on technology—they succeed because victims believe what they see or hear.

Why These Threats Are Hard to Detect

- Deepfakes and voice cloning can now be created with just a few minutes of sample video or audio

- AI can mimic writing styles convincingly, especially if it has access to internal communications or public profiles

- Traditional security tools like spam filters or antivirus programs don't detect emotional manipulation or synthetic voices

How to Defend Against AI-Based Attacks

1. **Don't Trust What You See or Hear Alone**

2. Treat unexpected videos or voice messages—even from familiar people—with skepticism, especially if they involve urgent financial actions or confidential data.

3. **Verify Through Secondary Channels**

4. If you receive an unusual request from a known individual:

   o Call them on a known phone number

   o Speak to them in person or through a secure video call

   o Use a company-approved communication platform to confirm

5. **Establish Verification Protocols**

   ○ Set internal rules: No fund transfers without two-person approval

   ○ Use code words or verification phrases in sensitive voice or video instructions

   ○ Use official channels (not WhatsApp, personal email, or SMS) for approvals

6. **Limit Public Exposure of Executives and Employees**

   ○ Don't overshare voice, video, or personal details of leaders on public platforms

   ○ Reduce unnecessary posting of leadership updates, presentations, and interviews unless securely managed

7. **Educate Employees Regularly**

8. Train your staff to:

   ○ Understand what deepfakes and AI threats are

   ○ Recognize red flags (unusual tone, timing, background noise, or urgent tone)

   ○ Report suspicious messages or content immediately

9. **Monitor Social Media and Mentions**

10. Companies should track fake or altered content appearing on social media or other platforms and respond promptly to misinformation.

Technology Can Help—but Awareness Is Key

There are emerging tools that can detect deepfakes or voice cloning, but they are still imperfect. For now, your best defense is critical thinking, multi-channel verification, and following strict business processes.

Real-World Example

In 2020, a fraudster used AI voice spoofing to impersonate a company's CEO and convince an employee to transfer $243,000 to a foreign supplier. The voice mimicked the CEO's German accent and tone so well that the employee didn't suspect anything—until the money was gone. This case was one of the first publicized AI voice frauds and triggered a wave of security reviews across the industry.

In Summary

AI-powered threats like deepfakes and voice spoofing represent the next level of social engineering. These aren't just technical challenges—they're psychological ones, targeting human trust and judgment. By combining awareness, clear protocols, and verification habits, professionals at all levels can protect themselves and their organizations against this new class of digital deception.

In the next chapter, we'll cover **Incident Reporting and Ticketing Systems**, explaining how and when to report security concerns, and why timely reporting is essential to minimize damage.

Chapter 44

Incident Reporting and Ticketing Systems: Responding Quickly When Things Go Wrong

No matter how strong your security measures are, incidents can still happen—whether it's a phishing email that was clicked, a suspicious login attempt, a device that went missing, or an internal application malfunction. The key is **how fast and effectively your organization responds.**

This chapter introduces the concepts of **incident reporting** and **ticketing systems**, explaining why timely, accurate reporting is essential, what employees should do when something goes wrong, and how IT and security teams manage incidents using structured workflows.

What Is an Incident in the Digital Workplace?

A **security incident** is any event that compromises—or has the potential to compromise—your systems, data, or operations. Examples include:

- Clicking on a suspicious link or attachment
- Receiving an impersonation email
- Detecting unauthorized access to systems
- Loss or theft of a company device
- Discovering malware or unusual computer behavior

196

- Accidentally sending sensitive data to the wrong person

Not all incidents are catastrophic, but even small ones can escalate quickly if ignored or mishandled.

Why Incident Reporting Matters

Employees are often the **first line of detection**. The sooner an issue is reported:

- The faster IT/security can investigate and contain the threat
- The more likely the organization can avoid data loss or legal consequences
- The easier it is to recover or reverse any damage
- Patterns can be identified (e.g., repeated phishing attempts from the same source)

Delays in reporting—even out of embarrassment or uncertainty—can cost time, money, and reputation.

What Should Be Reported?

If you're ever in doubt, report it. Typical situations to report include:

- Suspicious emails or messages, even if you didn't click
- Lost or stolen laptops, phones, USB drives, or access cards
- Malware or antivirus warnings
- Unexpected system behavior or error messages
- Unauthorized persons seen in restricted areas
- Files or documents you accidentally exposed or shared incorrectly
- Being tricked into giving credentials or sending money

How to Report an Incident

Most companies have a defined process for incident reporting. It typically involves:

1. **Submitting a Ticket** via the IT Helpdesk or Security Portal
   - Describe what happened, when, and on which device/account

- Attach screenshots or email headers if applicable

2. **Contacting the IT/Security Team Directly** (for urgent or high-risk incidents)
   - Call or message a designated contact or security hotline

3. **Filling Out a Security Incident Form** (if available)
   - For more detailed or formal submissions, especially in regulated industries

Best Practices for Employees

- Don't try to fix the issue yourself unless instructed
- Avoid deleting suspicious emails or files—quarantine or isolate them
- Provide as much detail as possible: time, system, context
- Stay available in case the IT or security team needs clarification
- Follow up if you don't receive acknowledgment of your report

What Happens After You Report

1. **Acknowledgment**

   You receive confirmation that your report or ticket has been received

2. **Initial Triage**

   The IT or security team assesses the severity and impact of the incident

3. **Investigation**

   Logs are reviewed, systems are scanned, and impacted users are identified

4. **Containment and Resolution**

   Threats are blocked, access is revoked, malware is removed, and patches are applied

5. **Communication and Closure**

   You may be asked for more information or notified of any action you need to take

6. **Post-Incident Review**

   The team may analyze what went wrong and update policies, training, or systems to prevent recurrence

The Role of Ticketing Systems

A **ticketing system** (like Freshservice, Jira, Zendesk, or ServiceNow) helps manage incidents by:

- Logging reports in a centralized location

- Assigning tasks to relevant teams

- Tracking resolution steps and timelines

- Providing audit trails for compliance or review

- Prioritizing based on urgency and impact

Tickets are also used for routine IT support (e.g., password resets, access requests), but security tickets are often flagged as urgent and may follow a different workflow.

Real-World Example

An employee receives an invoice from what looks like a regular supplier. Something seems off, so they report it to the security team. Upon investigation, it's found to be a phishing campaign targeting the entire finance department. Because the employee reported it quickly, the email was blocked across the company, and no funds were lost.

Fostering a Culture of Reporting

Organizations must:

- Make reporting channels clear and accessible

- Avoid blame—people should feel safe admitting mistakes

- Recognize and reward responsible behavior

- Provide feedback so employees know their reports were taken seriously

In Summary

Incident reporting isn't just an IT function—it's a shared responsibility across the organization. If something seems unusual, suspicious, or accidental, **report it early, accurately, and without fear**. You don't need to be an expert—you just need to act. Your quick response can make the difference between a minor issue and a major crisis.

In the next chapter, we'll look at **Smartphone Essentials: Setup, Use, and Mobile Security**

Chapter 45
Smartphone Essentials: Setup, Use, and Mobile Security

Smartphones have become an essential part of modern work life. From checking emails and attending virtual meetings to accessing business apps and approving workflows, mobile devices extend the digital workplace into our hands. But with that convenience comes a critical need for **awareness, responsibility, and security**.

This chapter focuses on how to set up, use, and secure smartphones—whether personal or company-issued—so that they enhance productivity without compromising personal data or organizational security.

Why Smartphones Matter in the Workplace

A smartphone is more than a communication tool. For many employees and managers, it serves as:

- An email and calendar hub
- A document viewer and editor
- A project and task management tool
- A virtual meeting and messaging platform
- A gateway to ERP, CRM, HR, and financial systems

With access to so much business-critical data, a compromised phone can become a major security threat.

Setting Up a Smartphone for Work Use

1. **Use a Separate Work Profile (If Available)**

   Many mobile operating systems (especially Android) allow you to create a separate work profile, keeping business apps and data isolated from personal use.

2. **Enroll in Mobile Device Management (MDM)**

   If your organization uses an MDM solution (like Microsoft Intune or VMware Workspace ONE), follow the enrollment instructions. MDM allows IT to:

   o Enforce security policies

   o Push updates

   o Remotely wipe data in case of loss or theft

   o Manage app access

3. **Install Only Approved Business Apps**

   Use only the official versions of business tools (email, ERP, CRM) from trusted app stores. Avoid using third-party alternatives that aren't IT-approved.

4. **Connect Through Secure Channels**

   Always use a VPN (Virtual Private Network) when connecting to company systems from outside trusted networks.

Best Practices for Secure Mobile Use

1. Lock Your Device Properly

- Use biometric authentication (fingerprint, face ID) or a strong passcode

- Avoid using simple patterns or 4-digit PINs

- Set your phone to auto-lock after a short period of inactivity

2. Keep the Operating System and Apps Updated

- Enable automatic updates

- Check regularly for app updates in the App Store or Google Play

- Remove apps you no longer use

3. Enable Remote Wipe and Device Tracking

- Activate features like "Find My iPhone" or "Find My Device"
- If the phone is lost or stolen, report it to IT and wipe it remotely if necessary

4. Be Cautious with Public Wi-Fi

- Avoid accessing work accounts or sensitive apps on open networks
- Use a VPN when working from cafes, airports, or public spaces

5. Be Mindful of App Permissions

- Review and restrict apps' access to location, contacts, camera, microphone, etc.
- Do not grant permissions unless absolutely necessary

6. Avoid Rooting or Jailbreaking Your Phone

- These actions disable built-in security features and make your phone vulnerable to malware

7. Backup Your Data Securely

- Use encrypted cloud backups
- Avoid storing work files in personal cloud services unless approved

8. Use Encrypted Messaging for Business Communication

- If permitted, apps like Microsoft Teams or Signal provide end-to-end encryption
- Avoid sending sensitive information via SMS or unencrypted platforms

Real-World Example

An employee used their personal phone to access the company's email system. The device had no password, and they accidentally left it in a taxi. Though the finder didn't unlock it, the company had to disable the account and review logs to ensure no data was accessed. Had the phone been enrolled in MDM with auto-lock and remote wipe, the response would've been faster and more effective.

Mobile Phishing and Messaging Scams

Smartphones are especially vulnerable to **smishing** (SMS-based phishing), WhatsApp scams, and fake app notifications. Always:

- Verify links before clicking
- Avoid installing apps via shared links—use official app stores only
- Report suspicious messages to IT

Etiquette and Professional Use of Smartphones

- Keep personal and business communications separate
- Don't take screenshots of confidential information unless necessary
- Use headphones during calls or meetings in public
- Turn off notifications during presentations or video conferences

In Summary

Smartphones are powerful tools for productivity—but they must be set up and used responsibly. Treat your phone like a portable office, with the same level of care you would give a laptop or desktop. By following simple practices—like locking your screen, using VPNs, and installing only approved apps—you keep your data, your organization, and yourself safe in the mobile-first workplace.

In next section we will cover Virtualization, Cloud Computing and Containerization.

PART 8

VIRTUALIZATION, CLOUD COMPUTING, AND CONTAINERIZATION

Chapter 46

Virtual Machines and Hypervisors: The Foundation of Modern IT Infrastructure

Virtualization is one of the most significant innovations in information technology. It allows businesses to run multiple virtual computers—called virtual machines (VMs)—on a single physical device. This improves server efficiency, reduces costs, and creates a flexible IT environment that can be scaled up or down as needed.

In this chapter, we'll explore how virtual machines work, what hypervisors do, and why understanding virtualization is important for modern business operations.

Why Virtualization Matters in Business

Before virtualization, each business application typically needed its own dedicated server. That meant:

- More physical machines to maintain

- Higher hardware and energy costs

- Limited flexibility when scaling services

With virtualization, multiple VMs can run side by side on a single physical server—each functioning as if it were a full computer with its own operating system and applications.

Virtualization is used to:

- Run multiple systems or apps on one server
- Test software in isolated environments
- Create development and training environments
- Manage disaster recovery more easily

What Is a Virtual Machine (VM)?

A **Virtual Machine** is a software-based simulation of a physical computer. It has:

- A virtual CPU
- Virtual memory (RAM)
- Virtual disk storage
- A virtual network card

From a user's perspective, a VM behaves just like a regular computer—but it's running inside a window or tab on a host system.

What Is a Hypervisor?

A **Hypervisor** is the software layer that creates and manages virtual machines. It handles the allocation of physical resources to each VM and keeps them isolated from each other.

There are two main types:

- **Type 1 (Bare Metal)**: Installed directly on the hardware (e.g., VMware ESXi, Microsoft Hyper-V, Xen)
- **Type 2 (Hosted)**: Runs as an application on an operating system (e.g., Oracle VirtualBox, VMware Workstation)

Hypervisors enable IT teams to deploy VMs quickly, manage them centrally, and recover or move them between servers with minimal downtime.

Benefits of Virtual Machines

1. **Cost Efficiency**

   Reduces hardware and power needs by consolidating systems onto fewer machines.

2. **Scalability**

   Easy to spin up new VMs for testing, development, or extra capacity.

3. **Isolation and Security**

   If one VM crashes or gets infected, it doesn't affect others running on the same host.

4. **Disaster Recovery and Backup**VMs can be quickly backed up, copied, or restored—speeding up disaster recovery efforts.

5. **Platform Independence**

   Run different operating systems on the same hardware (e.g., Linux and Windows together).

Master Proxmox Virtualization Like a Pro!

Turn your IT infrastructure into a high-performance virtualized powerhouse.

Real-World Example

A mid-size company used to maintain 10 physical servers for different departments—HR, Sales, Finance, and so on. By adopting VMware ESXi, they were able to consolidate all their services into 2 powerful physical servers running 15 virtual machines. This reduced energy consumption, improved system availability, and made it easier for the IT team to manage updates and backups.

Common Use Cases for VMs in the Workplace

- Running legacy applications that require old operating systems
- Creating isolated environments for software testing
- Deploying temporary systems for interns or contractors
- Simulating cyberattack scenarios for security training
- Training employees in safe, disposable environments

Risks and Considerations

While virtualization has many advantages, it must be managed carefully:

- Overloading a host with too many VMs can degrade performance
- Each VM needs proper security (firewall, updates, antivirus)
- Licensing and compliance must be maintained across all virtual instances

Getting Started with Virtualization (for Non-IT Users)

Even non-technical professionals can benefit from understanding virtualization:

- You may use a VM during training or product demos
- Developers often request VMs for isolated testing environments
- Some companies use VMs to securely run high-risk or untrusted software

Ask your IT team if virtualization is being used in your organization, and learn how you can interact with these environments safely and effectively.

In Summary

Virtual machines and hypervisors are the backbone of efficient, flexible IT environments. They allow organizations to run more with less—saving space, time, and money. Whether you're in operations, development, or management, understanding how virtualization works helps you make smarter decisions when it comes to IT planning and resource allocation.

In the next chapter, we'll explore **Cloud Platforms and Service Models (IaaS, PaaS, SaaS)**, so you can understand how cloud computing builds on virtualization to deliver scalable and on-demand digital services.

Chapter 47
Cloud Platforms and Service Models (IaaS, PaaS, SaaS): Understanding the Layers of the Cloud

Cloud computing has transformed how organizations deploy, scale, and manage technology. It allows businesses to access computing power, storage, applications, and infrastructure over the internet—on-demand and without managing physical hardware.

This chapter explores the most widely used cloud platforms and explains the three core service models—**IaaS (Infrastructure as a Service)**, **PaaS (Platform as a Service)**, and **SaaS (Software as a Service)**—so you can understand their roles, differences, and relevance to modern business environments.

Why Cloud Computing Is Important

Before the cloud, businesses had to buy, install, and maintain their own servers and software. This meant high upfront costs, long setup times, and complex maintenance.

With the cloud:

- You pay only for what you use (subscription or usage-based pricing)

- Services are available instantly and accessible from anywhere

- Maintenance, security, and updates are handled by cloud providers

- Businesses gain agility—scaling up or down as needed

Whether you're running a small business or a global enterprise, cloud services now underpin most digital operations.

Popular Cloud Providers

The leading platforms include:

- **Amazon Web Services (AWS)** – Offers a wide range of cloud services

- **Microsoft Azure** – Strong in hybrid cloud and Microsoft ecosystem integration

- **Google Cloud Platform (GCP)** – Known for analytics, AI, and container services

- Others: Oracle Cloud, IBM Cloud, Alibaba Cloud

Each platform offers hundreds of services—from data storage and compute power to machine learning and security tools.

The Three Main Service Models

Understanding IaaS, PaaS, and SaaS is key to making informed decisions about cloud adoption.

1. Infrastructure as a Service (IaaS)

IaaS provides the **fundamental computing resources**—servers, storage, and networking—over the internet. It gives businesses control over the operating system, applications, and data, without worrying about physical hardware.

Example Providers: AWS EC2, Microsoft Azure Virtual Machines, Google Compute Engine

Common Use Cases:

- Hosting websites and applications

- Running custom enterprise software

- Creating development and testing environments

- Backup and disaster recovery

What You Manage:

- Applications, data, runtime, and OS

What the Provider Manages:

- Virtual machines, storage, networking, and physical infrastructure

2. Platform as a Service (PaaS)

PaaS provides a **ready-to-use development environment** that lets developers build, test, and deploy applications without managing servers or databases.

Example Providers: Microsoft Azure App Services, Google App Engine, Heroku

Common Use Cases:

- Developing web and mobile applications
- Automating software deployment pipelines
- Scaling applications without worrying about infrastructure

What You Manage:

- Application code and configuration

What the Provider Manages:

- Runtime, middleware, OS, servers, and storage

PaaS is ideal for developers who want to focus on writing code—not managing infrastructure.

3. Software as a Service (SaaS)

SaaS delivers **complete applications over the internet**, which are ready to use. Users access these apps through browsers or mobile apps, and everything—from hosting to updates—is handled by the provider.

Example Providers:

- Google Workspace (Gmail, Docs, Sheets)
- Microsoft 365 (Outlook, Teams, Word, Excel)
- Salesforce (CRM)
- Zoom, Dropbox, Slack

Common Use Cases:

- Email and collaboration
- Customer relationship management (CRM)

- Document sharing and editing
- Project management and HR systems

What You Manage:

- Only your user settings and data

What the Provider Manages:

- Everything else (application, servers, storage, security)

SaaS is the most user-friendly and widely adopted model in most organizations.

Real-World Example

A startup begins by using Gmail and Google Drive (SaaS). As they grow, they deploy their app using Google App Engine (PaaS), allowing developers to focus on code. Later, they migrate to AWS EC2 (IaaS) for more control over the environment as their app becomes more complex.

Each stage reflects increasing control—and complexity.

Comparing the Models

Feature	IaaS	PaaS	SaaS
Control	High	Medium	Low
Responsibility	User-managed OS/apps	Focus on code	Use the software as-is
Flexibility	Very flexible	Limited by platform	Fixed functionality
Technical Expertise	High	Medium	Low

Security and Cost Considerations

- **IaaS** offers more control but requires strong internal security management

- **PaaS** reduces operational overhead but may limit customization

- **SaaS** is easiest to use, but data privacy and integration should be reviewed

Always consider compliance, data sovereignty, and vendor reliability before selecting a cloud service.

In Summary

Cloud service models—Infrastructure (IaaS), Platform (PaaS), and Software (SaaS)—offer different levels of control, flexibility, and responsibility. Understanding the difference helps you choose the right tool for your business goals, technical capability, and budget.

In the next chapter, we'll explore **Public, Private, and Hybrid Cloud**, so you can understand how organizations decide where to host their data and how to balance security, performance, and cost.

Chapter 48
Public, Private, and Hybrid Cloud Explained: Choosing the Right Environment for Your Business

When moving to the cloud, one of the first strategic decisions an organization faces is choosing the **type of cloud deployment**: public, private, or hybrid. Each option has its own strengths, limitations, and use cases depending on business needs, data sensitivity, budget, and regulatory requirements.

This chapter breaks down these three models so you can understand their key characteristics, how they work, and how businesses use them in real-world scenarios.

Public Cloud

The public cloud is a model where computing resources—such as servers, storage, and applications—are hosted by a third-party provider and shared among multiple customers (also known as tenants).

Examples of public cloud providers include Amazon Web Services (AWS), Microsoft Azure, and Google Cloud Platform.

Key Characteristics of Public Cloud

Scalable: Instantly add or remove resources as needed

Pay-as-you-go pricing: Pay only for what you use

Managed infrastructure: The provider handles maintenance, hardware, and updates

Accessible from anywhere: Services are available via the internet

Common Use Cases

Startups and small businesses hosting websites and applications

Organizations needing disaster recovery or backup solutions

Development and testing environments

Businesses with unpredictable workloads that need to scale on demand

Challenges

Less control over the physical infrastructure

Shared environment may raise concerns over data isolation and compliance

Internet dependency—service interruptions can affect access

Private Cloud

A private cloud is a cloud environment used exclusively by one organization. It may be hosted on-premise in the company's data center or offsite by a third-party provider but remains dedicated to a single tenant.

Key Characteristics of Private Cloud

Higher control and customization: Configure infrastructure to meet specific needs

Enhanced security and compliance: Ideal for businesses in regulated industries

Dedicated resources: Not shared with other organizations

Common Use Cases

Financial institutions managing confidential transactions

Government agencies handling sensitive data

Large enterprises running mission-critical applications that require custom architecture

Organizations with strict regulatory and data sovereignty requirements

Challenges

Higher upfront and operational costs

Longer setup and maintenance times

Requires skilled IT staff to manage infrastructure

Hybrid Cloud

A hybrid cloud combines public and private clouds, allowing data and applications to move between the two environments. This setup offers the flexibility of the public cloud and the control of the private cloud.

Key Characteristics of Hybrid Cloud

Balance between scalability and control

Improved risk management—keep sensitive data in private cloud, use public cloud for less sensitive workloads

Enables gradual migration from legacy systems to the cloud

Business continuity—if one environment fails, the other can take over

Common Use Cases

Companies with existing on-premise infrastructure wanting to expand into cloud gradually

Retail businesses managing spikes in demand during seasonal sales

Healthcare providers needing to store patient data privately but access services online

Any organization that wants to optimize cost while meeting compliance needs

Multi-Cloud vs. Hybrid Cloud

It's also worth distinguishing between **multi-cloud** and **hybrid cloud**:

- **Hybrid Cloud** uses a mix of public and private cloud platforms working together

- **Multi-Cloud** involves using multiple public cloud providers (e.g., AWS and Azure) for different services, without necessarily integrating them

Real-World Example

A logistics company runs its core transportation system in a private cloud to maintain full control and ensure compliance. It uses the public cloud for analytics and mobile apps used by drivers and customers. The two environments are integrated, making it a classic hybrid cloud setup.

Factors to Consider When Choosing a Cloud Model

- **Data Sensitivity**: Where is your most sensitive data stored?

- **Compliance**: Are there legal or industry-specific rules about data location or access?

- **Budget**: Can you afford the capital and operational costs of private cloud infrastructure?

- **Scalability Needs**: Do you need to scale resources quickly or seasonally?

- **In-House Expertise**: Do you have the right IT skills to manage the environment?

In Summary

Choosing between public, private, and hybrid cloud depends on your organization's size, security needs, compliance obligations, and growth strategy. Many businesses today adopt hybrid models to get the best of both worlds—scalability from public cloud, and control from private infrastructure.

In the next chapter, we'll explore **Containers and Kubernetes**, which are essential technologies used to build, deploy, and manage applications in modern cloud-native environments.

Chapter 49
Containers and Kubernetes: Powering Modern Application Deployment

As businesses adopt cloud technologies and move toward more agile development, the need for flexible, efficient, and scalable application deployment has grown. Traditional virtual machines are powerful but can be heavy and slow to start. That's where **containers** and **Kubernetes** come in.

In this chapter, we'll explore what containers are, how they differ from virtual machines, and how Kubernetes orchestrates containers at scale. Understanding these technologies gives you insight into how modern apps are built, deployed, and scaled in real-time.

What Are Containers?

A **container** is a lightweight, portable unit that packages an application and everything it needs to run—code, runtime, libraries, and dependencies—into a single bundle. Containers ensure that applications run consistently regardless of the environment.

Unlike virtual machines, which include a full guest operating system, containers share the host OS kernel. This makes them much faster and more efficient.

Key Characteristics of Containers

- Lightweight: Use less memory and start faster than virtual machines
- Portable: Run the same on any system that supports the container runtime
- Isolated: Each container operates in its own environment, avoiding conflicts
- Scalable: Easily create multiple instances of an application

Popular Container Platforms

- **Docker**: The most widely used container platform for developers and IT teams
- **Podman**: An alternative to Docker, often used for its daemonless architecture
- **LXC/LXD**: System containers used in advanced enterprise scenarios

Real-World Example of Container Use

Imagine a software company developing a new customer portal. Developers work on different modules—login, dashboard, reporting—each in its own container. These can be tested independently, run in isolation, and deployed to production with consistency and speed.

Instead of shipping software that works "on one server but not another," containers guarantee consistent behavior across environments—on a developer's laptop, in testing, and in the cloud.

What Is Kubernetes?

While containers are powerful, managing hundreds or thousands of them manually is difficult. **Kubernetes** (often abbreviated as K8s) is an open-source platform for **automating the deployment, scaling, and operation of containerized applications**.

Kubernetes helps you:

- Deploy applications in containers across a cluster of servers

- Automatically restart failed containers

- Scale applications up or down based on demand

- Load balance traffic to maintain performance

- Roll out updates with minimal downtime

Core Concepts in Kubernetes

- **Pod**: The smallest unit in Kubernetes—one or more containers that share resources

- **Node**: A server (virtual or physical) where pods run

- **Cluster**: A group of nodes managed by Kubernetes

- **Service**: A stable endpoint for accessing a group of pods

- **Deployment**: Defines how containers should be deployed, updated, and scaled

Use Cases for Kubernetes

- Hosting large-scale web apps that need auto-scaling

- Managing microservices architecture (breaking apps into small, modular components)

- Running DevOps pipelines for continuous integration and deployment (CI/CD)

- Operating in hybrid or multi-cloud environments

Containers vs. Virtual Machines

Feature	Containers	Virtual Machines
Startup Time	Seconds	Minutes
Size	Megabytes	Gigabytes
OS Dependency	Shares host OS	Full guest OS per VM
Portability	Highly portable	Less portable
Use Case	Microservices, DevOps	Legacy apps, isolated OS

Security and Monitoring

While containers offer isolation, they share the host OS, so misconfigurations can lead to vulnerabilities. Best practices include:

- Scanning container images for vulnerabilities
- Limiting permissions (avoid root containers)
- Using signed images and trusted registries
- Applying network policies to control traffic between containers
- Using monitoring tools like Prometheus, Grafana, or Datadog to track performance and health

In Summary

Containers and Kubernetes are driving the future of software deployment. They allow teams to build, test, and deliver applications faster, more reliably, and at scale. Even if you're not a developer or system administrator, understanding how containers work helps you appreciate how your business software is being delivered and maintained in today's cloud-first world.

In the next chapter, we'll cover **Backup, Disaster Recovery (DR), and Business Continuity**, helping you understand how organizations protect critical systems and recover quickly when disaster strikes.

Chapter 50
Backup, Disaster Recovery, and Business Continuity: Preparing for the Unexpected

No matter how secure, modern, or well-managed your IT systems are, failures and disruptions are inevitable. A server may crash, a file may be deleted by mistake, ransomware could encrypt critical data, or a natural disaster might take your systems offline. The difference between a minor inconvenience and a business-halting crisis is how well you're prepared.

This chapter focuses on three essential practices that every business—large or small—must understand and implement: **Backup, Disaster Recovery (DR)**, and **Business Continuity (BC)**.

Why Backup, DR, and Business Continuity Matter

Organizations today are more dependent on digital systems than ever before. A data loss incident or prolonged downtime can mean:

- Financial loss due to disrupted operations

- Reputational damage with customers and partners

- Regulatory penalties if sensitive data is lost

- Permanent data loss affecting future decision-making

Proper planning ensures that you can recover data quickly, resume operations with minimal disruption, and maintain trust.

1. Backup: The Safety Net

Backup is the process of creating copies of your data so you can restore it if the original is lost, corrupted, or deleted.

Best Practices for Backups

- **Regular Scheduling**: Automate backups on a daily, weekly, or real-time basis depending on business need

- **Multiple Locations**: Keep at least one copy offsite or in the cloud

- **Versioning**: Maintain multiple versions of files to protect against unwanted changes

- **Encryption**: Ensure backups are encrypted to prevent unauthorized access

- **Testing**: Periodically test backups to verify they can be restored when needed

Common Types of Backups

- **Full Backup**: Copies all data

- **Incremental Backup**: Backs up only changes since the last backup

- **Differential Backup**: Backs up changes since the last full backup

Real-World Example

An employee accidentally deletes a folder containing customer invoices. Thanks to daily automated cloud backups, IT restores the folder within an hour with no data loss or business impact.

2. Disaster Recovery: Bringing Systems Back Online

Disaster Recovery (DR) refers to the strategy and processes used to recover IT systems and data after a catastrophic event such as:

- Server failure

- Cyberattack (e.g., ransomware)

- Natural disasters (e.g., fire, flood)

- Power outages or hardware failure

DR focuses on **restoring technical systems**, such as:

- File servers and databases

- Virtual machines and cloud infrastructure

- ERP, CRM, and business applications

Key Terms

- **RTO (Recovery Time Objective)**: How quickly you need to restore operations after a disruption

- **RPO (Recovery Point Objective)**: The maximum acceptable amount of data loss measured in time (e.g., "no more than 15 minutes of data")

Tools for Disaster Recovery

- Cloud-based DR services (e.g., Azure Site Recovery, AWS Backup)

- Snapshot and image-based backups

- Redundant systems and failover configurations

- Virtual machine replication across regions

3. Business Continuity: Keeping the Business Running

Business Continuity (BC) is a broader strategy than DR. It ensures that **essential business functions continue**, even if IT systems are down. It includes:

- Communication plans for employees and customers

- Alternative work arrangements (e.g., remote work if the office is closed)

- Manual procedures for critical operations

- Access to vital data, whether online or offline

Business Continuity Plan (BCP) Components

- Identification of critical processes and systems

- Risk assessment and business impact analysis

- Roles and responsibilities during a crisis

- Step-by-step procedures for maintaining operations

- Contact lists and emergency communication templates

Real-World Example

A company's main data center goes offline due to a fire. Their cloud-based ERP system allows remote teams to continue processing orders. Meanwhile, customer service switches to mobile apps and VoIP tools. Regular backups and a solid continuity plan enable business operations to continue with minimal disruption.

Modern Trends in DR and BC

- **Cloud-native DR solutions** offer flexibility and reduce reliance on physical infrastructure

- **Hybrid DR strategies** combine cloud and on-premise tools for redundancy

- **Business Impact Analysis (BIA)** is increasingly integrated into IT planning

- **Work-from-anywhere policies** are becoming standard in BC planning

Employee's Role in Recovery Planning

- Save files only to designated systems or cloud folders

- Understand basic data recovery procedures

- Report issues promptly

- Know who to contact in case of an outage or emergency

In Summary

Backup, disaster recovery, and business continuity aren't just IT responsibilities—they're business imperatives. Whether you're managing systems, leading a team, or simply using company data in your daily role, understanding these strategies helps you act responsibly, reduce risks, and support organizational resilience.

In the next Section , we'll explore **Automation, AI and the Future Work.**

PART 9

AUTOMATION, AI, AND THE FUTURE OF WORK

Chapter 51

Workflow Automation Tools: Simplifying Repetitive Work with Zapier, Power Automate, n8n, and More

In every organization, there are dozens of small, repetitive tasks—sending emails, copying data between systems, updating spreadsheets, notifying teams about updates. These tasks may seem minor on their own, but over time, they consume hours of valuable human effort. **Workflow automation** tools are designed to eliminate this burden by connecting apps and automating actions across platforms.

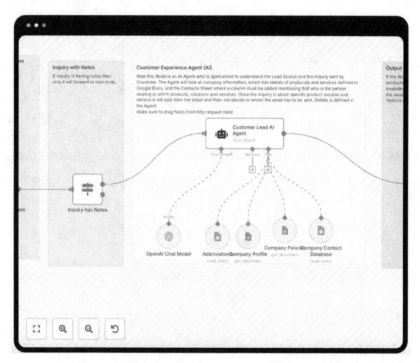

This chapter introduces you to the concept of workflow automation, how it works, and how tools like **Zapier, Power Automate, n8n, make.com, and Activepieces** are changing the way businesses operate.

What Is Workflow Automation?

Workflow automation is the process of setting up rules or triggers that automatically perform actions across your digital tools. These actions often follow an "if this, then that" pattern. For example:

- If a new customer fills out a web form → send them a welcome email

- If a file is added to a shared folder → create a task in a project management app

- If a sale is made in the eCommerce platform → update the CRM and notify the sales team

By automating these processes, you reduce manual errors, save time, and ensure consistency.

Popular Workflow Automation Tools

1. **Zapier:** User-friendly and designed for non-developers, Zapier connects thousands of apps like Gmail, Google Sheets, Trello, and Slack. It works well for simple, linear automations.

2. **Microsoft Power Automate:** Part of the Microsoft ecosystem, Power Automate is ideal for automating tasks across Office 365, SharePoint, Dynamics, and Teams. It supports advanced workflows, approvals, and integrations with hundreds of business applications.

3. **n8n:** An open-source, self-hosted automation platform built for privacy and flexibility. It supports complex flows, custom scripts, and API connections, and is favored by developers and tech-savvy teams.

4. **Make.com (formerly Integromat):** Offers a visual builder for complex automation scenarios. Known for powerful logic handling, error management, and support for advanced APIs.

5. **Activepieces:** A newer open-source alternative to Zapier. It's suitable for building automations on-premises or in secure environments where cloud-based tools may not be appropriate.

Real-World Examples of Automation in Action

- HR teams automate onboarding: When a new employee is added to the system, an automated workflow sends a welcome email, adds them to the HR system, creates accounts in collaboration tools, and notifies the manager.

- Sales teams integrate leads: A lead from a Facebook form triggers the creation of a CRM entry, sends a follow-up email, and schedules a task for the sales rep.

- Finance departments streamline approvals: When an invoice is submitted, Power Automate routes it to the right approver, sends reminders, and updates the payment status in the ERP.

N8n & AI Powered Automation Mastery Build AI-Powered Automations with N8n – Self-Hosting, Docker, Templates, and Make vs N8n	

Benefits of Workflow Automation

- Saves time by eliminating repetitive manual steps
- Improves accuracy and reduces human error
- Increases consistency across business processes
- Frees up employees for higher-value, strategic work
- Enhances visibility into task status and ownership

Common Use Cases in Daily Work

- Email alerts for task assignments

- Auto-syncing data between Google Sheets and your ERP

- Generating reports on a schedule

- Automating customer feedback collection

- Managing social media posting

Key Considerations Before Automating

- Start with processes that are repetitive, well-defined, and rules-based

- Map out the current process before building an automation

- Always test with sample data before rolling out

- Ensure compliance with company data policies, especially when using third-party tools

- Monitor automations regularly for errors or broken steps

Get n8n

Build AI-Powered Automations with N8n

n8n.syncbricks.com

In Summary

Workflow automation tools help individuals and teams eliminate tedious work and focus on what matters most. Whether you're a non-technical employee using Zapier or a power user building custom flows in n8n, automation is within reach. These tools represent a major step toward smarter, leaner, and more productive digital work environments.

In the next chapter, we'll introduce **AI for Professionals**, helping you understand what artificial intelligence is, what it can (and can't) do, and why it's becoming a core part of every workplace.

Chapter 52

Introduction to AI for Professionals: What It Is, How It Works, and Why It Matters

Artificial Intelligence (AI) is no longer a concept reserved for science fiction or tech giants. It's now woven into the everyday operations of modern businesses—helping teams analyze data, automate decisions, serve customers, and unlock new efficiencies. As a professional, understanding the fundamentals of AI is becoming just as important as knowing how to use email or spreadsheets.

This chapter provides a clear, practical introduction to AI—explaining what it is, how it works, and how it's being applied across industries and business functions.

What Is Artificial Intelligence?

Artificial Intelligence refers to the ability of machines or software to perform tasks that typically require human intelligence. This includes:

- Understanding language

- Recognizing patterns

- Making predictions

- Learning from data

- Automating decision-making

Unlike traditional software, which follows predefined instructions, AI systems can adapt, improve, and even make recommendations or decisions based on data and context.

Types of AI You May Encounter at Work

Narrow AI (also called Weak AI)

Focused on a single task. Most AI tools today are narrow AI.

Examples: Email spam filters, recommendation engines, facial recognition, chatbots

Generative AI

Creates new content (text, images, audio, code) based on patterns it has learned from large datasets.

Examples: ChatGPT for text, DALL·E for images, GitHub Copilot for coding

Machine Learning (ML)

A subset of AI where systems learn from data instead of being explicitly programmed.

Examples: Predictive sales forecasting, customer churn modeling, fraud detection

Key Characteristics of AI

- Data-driven: AI systems improve over time as they are exposed to more data

- Pattern recognition: AI excels at spotting trends humans might miss

- Automation: AI can perform tasks faster and at scale, freeing up human capacity

- Context-aware: Some AI tools understand and adapt based on the situation

Common Business Use Cases

Customer Support

AI chatbots handle common questions 24/7, escalate issues to human agents, and provide instant responses.

Marketing

AI analyzes customer behavior to personalize email campaigns, segment audiences, and optimize ad spend.

Operations

AI automates inventory forecasting, demand planning, and logistics routing to reduce waste and improve efficiency.

Human Resources

AI helps screen job applicants, schedule interviews, and even assist with employee sentiment analysis.

Finance

AI tools detect unusual transactions, generate financial summaries, and support budgeting with predictive analytics.

Real-World Example

A mid-sized eCommerce company uses AI to recommend products to customers based on their browsing and purchase history. Within six months, the average order value increases by 15%. They also deploy a customer service chatbot that resolves 40% of support tickets without human intervention—cutting costs and improving response times.

Benefits of AI for Professionals

- Improves decision-making by surfacing data insights quickly
- Reduces time spent on repetitive tasks
- Enhances productivity with tools like AI writing assistants or data analysis bots
- Creates opportunities for innovation in how services are delivered and managed

Challenges and Considerations

- Data quality: AI is only as good as the data it learns from
- Bias and fairness: Poorly trained models can reflect or amplify human bias
- Overreliance: AI should support—not replace—critical human judgment
- Security: Sensitive data used in AI systems must be protected

Is AI Coming for Your Job?

AI is more likely to **augment** jobs than replace them. While it may automate routine tasks, it also creates new opportunities for strategic work, creative problem-solving, and innovation. Professionals who understand how to work alongside AI—and use it effectively—will have a significant advantage.

In Summary

AI is no longer an emerging trend—it's an active part of the modern workplace. Whether you're in finance, marketing, HR, or operations, understanding how AI works and where it fits gives you an edge. You don't need to become a data scientist to benefit from AI—but you do need to be aware, open, and ready to adapt.

In the next chapter, we'll explore **Low-Code Platforms for Business Users**, a fast-growing trend that empowers professionals to build apps, automate workflows, and solve problems—without writing traditional code.

Chapter 53
Low-Code Platforms for Business Users: Build Without Being a Developer

Traditionally, creating software applications or automating internal workflows required skilled programmers writing complex code. But with the rise of **low-code platforms**, non-developers—often called "citizen developers"—can now build powerful business applications using visual interfaces, drag-and-drop components, and logic-based rules.

This chapter explains what low-code platforms are, how they differ from traditional software development, and how business users across departments can use them to solve problems, build tools, and digitize operations without writing a single line of code.

What Is a Low-Code Platform?

A low-code platform provides a graphical user interface (GUI) for designing applications and automations. It reduces the need for hand-coding by offering:

- Pre-built components (forms, workflows, connectors)

- Drag-and-drop logic builders

- Integration with databases and APIs

- Built-in deployment and access control

The goal is to make app development more accessible—so that professionals in HR, finance, operations, sales, and other areas can build tools tailored to their needs without relying entirely on IT departments.

How It Differs from No-Code

While both terms are sometimes used interchangeably, they are slightly different:

- **No-code platforms** are designed for users with zero technical skills

- **Low-code platforms** are more flexible and may require minimal scripting or understanding of data structures

In many organizations, low-code platforms strike a balance—easy enough for non-engineers, but powerful enough for IT to support and scale securely.

Popular Low-Code Platforms

- **Microsoft Power Apps** – A part of Microsoft Power Platform, tightly integrated with Office 365, SharePoint, and Dynamics

- **OutSystems** – Enterprise-grade platform for full-scale apps and systems

- **AppSheet (by Google)** – Build apps from spreadsheets or databases without coding

- **Mendix** – Supports rapid development and deployment across industries

- **Glide, Retool, and Zoho Creator** – Popular in small businesses and startups

Common Use Cases

Internal Tools

Create leave request apps, inventory dashboards, approval workflows, or onboarding trackers.

Data Collection and Reporting

Build mobile apps to collect field data, conduct audits, or generate real-time reports.

Customer Interfaces

Develop simple portals for support tickets, feedback collection, or appointment scheduling.

Process Automation

Automate invoice approvals, employee training checklists, or budget submission workflows.

Real-World Example

A retail company's HR department uses Power Apps to replace its outdated paper-based onboarding process. With no formal coding knowledge, they create a digital form that captures employee information, triggers background checks, and updates the HR database—all within a few days. What once took weeks is now automated and fully digital.

Benefits of Low-Code for Business Users

- Empowers non-technical teams to solve problems independently
- Reduces bottlenecks on IT departments
- Accelerates digital transformation by enabling rapid prototyping and deployment
- Encourages innovation and process improvement at the ground level
- Promotes a culture of continuous improvement and agility

Key Features to Look For

- Integration with your existing tools (Microsoft 365, Google Workspace, ERP systems)
- User access control and security settings
- Mobile responsiveness
- Workflow automation capabilities
- Data storage and reporting features

IT's Role in Supporting Low-Code Development

While low-code platforms empower business users, IT teams still play an essential role:

- Approving and managing platforms
- Setting governance policies and user roles
- Ensuring data security and compliance
- Supporting complex integrations with legacy systems

Risks and Best Practices

- **Shadow IT**: Unmonitored tools built without IT involvement can create risk. Ensure transparency.

- **Data integrity**: Apps must use secure and approved data sources.

- **Scalability**: Tools should be reviewed periodically to ensure they meet growing demands.

- **Training**: Offer training and templates to guide users in building effective solutions.

In Summary

Low-code platforms are transforming how problems get solved in the workplace. By enabling business users to build tools and automate tasks without programming skills, organizations become more agile, efficient, and digitally empowered. Whether you're an HR manager building a leave tracker or a sales team automating reporting, low-code is a powerful addition to your toolkit.

In the next chapter, we'll explore **Prompt Engineering and AI Models**, showing how professionals can get the most from AI tools like ChatGPT by crafting effective instructions and use-case-based prompts.

Chapter 54
Prompt Engineering and AI Models: Getting the Best Out of Tools Like ChatGPT

As AI tools like ChatGPT, Claude, and Google Gemini become integrated into daily business workflows, a new skill is emerging: **prompt engineering**. It's not about programming—it's about learning how to ask AI the right questions to get accurate, relevant, and valuable answers.

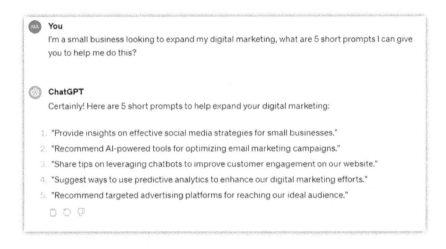

This chapter introduces you to the concept of prompt engineering, explains how AI language models work in simple terms, and shows how professionals across roles—whether in HR, marketing, operations, or leadership—can use prompts effectively to automate tasks, generate ideas, and solve problems.

What Is Prompt Engineering?

Prompt engineering is the practice of crafting effective instructions or questions for AI tools to generate useful responses. Since AI doesn't "understand" in the way humans do, the **quality of the prompt** determines the quality of the output.

Poor prompt:

"Write a report."

Better prompt:

"Write a one-page summary for a monthly sales report showing total revenue, top 3 performing products, and comparison to last month's numbers."

A well-structured prompt gives context, sets expectations, and guides the AI toward your goal.

Understanding How AI Models Work

AI tools like ChatGPT are built on **large language models (LLMs)**. These models are trained on massive amounts of text data to learn:

- Grammar and sentence structure

- Common patterns in conversation and writing

- Associations between topics, concepts, and styles

They do not "think" or "know" in the human sense but are very good at predicting the most likely next words in a sentence based on your prompt.

Types of AI Models Used in Prompt Engineering

- **Chat-based models** (e.g., ChatGPT, Claude, Gemini): Used for text generation, summarization, Q&A, ideation

- **Image generation models** (e.g., DALL·E, Midjourney): Create visuals from text prompts

- **Code generation models** (e.g., GitHub Copilot): Help developers write and troubleshoot code

- **Speech models** (e.g., ElevenLabs, PlayHT): Generate synthetic voice or transcribe spoken content

Key Elements of an Effective Prompt

1. **Clarity**: Be specific about what you want

2. **Context**: Provide background, goals, audience, or examples

3. **Constraints**: Set boundaries like word count, tone, or format

4. **Role-based framing**: Ask the AI to "act as" a particular professional (e.g., "Act as a cybersecurity consultant and explain…")

Examples by Use Case

Marketing

Prompt: "Write a promotional email for a new fitness app targeting working professionals aged 25–40. Keep it energetic and persuasive."

HR

Prompt: "Create a draft onboarding checklist for remote employees in a SaaS company, including equipment, tools, and policies."

Operations

Prompt: "Generate a step-by-step SOP for handling supplier invoice disputes in a retail company."

Leadership

Prompt: "Summarize the key lessons from the book 'Good to Great' in bullet points for a leadership workshop."

AI Prompt Templates You Can Reuse

- "Summarize [topic] in simple terms suitable for [audience]."
- "Create a table comparing [option A] and [option B] based on [criteria]."
- "List 10 blog ideas on [topic] for [industry/profession]."
- "Draft a policy on [topic] for a company of [size/type]."
- "Generate meeting agenda for [topic], with time estimates and discussion points."

Best Practices for Prompt Engineering

- Test and refine: Try different versions and see which gives better results
- Add examples: If you want a specific format, show a sample in your prompt

- Use follow-up prompts: You can ask the AI to revise, expand, or improve the initial output

- Avoid overloading: Long and unclear prompts confuse the model—break them into smaller parts

- Stay aware: Always verify facts—AI can occasionally generate incorrect or fabricated information (known as hallucination)

Limitations and Ethical Use

- AI tools should not replace expert opinion, especially in legal, financial, or medical matters

- Do not input sensitive company data into public AI platforms unless approved

- Always credit or disclose AI-generated content in professional and academic settings when required

Real-World Example

A team of content creators uses ChatGPT to generate first drafts of product descriptions. By standardizing prompts that include product type, target audience, and key features, they reduce writing time by 60% and maintain consistent tone and quality across hundreds of products.

In Summary

Prompt engineering is a critical digital skill that empowers professionals to unlock the full potential of AI tools. By learning how to give clear, strategic instructions, you can transform these tools into valuable assistants—for writing, research, planning, and problem-solving.

In the next chapter, we'll explore **AI in Business: Real-World Applications**, highlighting how AI is reshaping industries and specific departments with practical examples you can relate to and learn from.

Chapter 55
AI in Business: Real-World Applications Across Departments and Industries

Artificial Intelligence is no longer a buzzword—it's a practical, results-driven force behind many of the tools, platforms, and strategies used in businesses today. From improving customer service to predicting market trends and optimizing supply chains, AI is quietly working behind the scenes to drive performance and innovation.

This chapter explores real-world examples of how AI is being used across different business functions and industries. Whether you're in HR, finance, marketing, operations, or executive leadership, understanding how AI is applied helps you identify opportunities to improve efficiency, cut costs, and deliver better experiences.

AI in Customer Support

AI-powered chatbots and virtual assistants are now capable of resolving basic support tickets, answering FAQs, and routing requests to human agents when needed. These tools are available 24/7 and improve response time while reducing the workload on support teams.

Examples

- E-commerce sites use chatbots to answer delivery or return policy questions

- IT helpdesks automate password reset processes through AI chat

- Airlines provide real-time flight updates and rebooking options via AI assistants

AI in Sales and Marketing

AI helps businesses understand customer behavior, personalize content, and optimize campaigns. Predictive analytics tools use past customer data to forecast future buying patterns and lead scoring models help prioritize sales efforts.

Examples

- AI tools like HubSpot and Salesforce Einstein predict which leads are most likely to convert

- Email marketing platforms recommend send times and subject lines that improve open rates

- Ad platforms (like Google and Facebook) use AI to target the right audience with the right message

AI in Human Resources

AI is transforming how companies attract, hire, train, and retain employees. It automates repetitive tasks and offers deeper insights into workforce trends.

Examples

- Resume screening tools rank applicants based on job descriptions and past hiring success

- AI-based surveys analyze employee sentiment and predict turnover risk

- Learning platforms recommend personalized training based on performance or goals

AI in Finance and Accounting

AI improves financial forecasting, expense tracking, and fraud detection by recognizing patterns that might be missed by human reviewers.

Examples

- AI scans transactions to flag suspicious activity or anomalies

- Financial dashboards predict cash flow based on historical spending and seasonality

- Invoice processing is automated using OCR (Optical Character Recognition) and ML

AI in Supply Chain and Operations

In logistics and manufacturing, AI improves forecasting accuracy, inventory management, and route optimization.

Examples

- Retailers use AI to automatically reorder stock based on predictive demand

- Delivery companies optimize driver routes to reduce fuel costs

- AI models help manufacturers predict equipment failures and schedule maintenance

AI in Executive Decision-Making

Executives use AI-powered analytics platforms to track KPIs, identify trends, and simulate different business scenarios. Rather than replacing decision-makers, AI enhances their ability to make data-informed choices.

Examples

- CEOs use real-time dashboards for financial performance, HR metrics, and customer feedback

- Scenario planning tools forecast the impact of pricing changes or new product launches

- AI provides risk assessments for entering new markets or investing in new technology

Industry-Specific Applications

Healthcare

AI assists in diagnostics, patient monitoring, and personalized treatment plans.

Retail

AI predicts buying patterns, optimizes pricing, and enhances product recommendations.

Education

AI personalizes learning, tracks progress, and automates grading and feedback.

Legal

AI speeds up contract review and case law analysis.

Construction

AI forecasts project delays, tracks safety compliance, and analyzes construction site footage.

Benefits of AI Adoption

- Faster decision-making

- Increased operational efficiency

- Better customer and employee experience

- Cost savings through automation

- Competitive advantage in a data-driven economy

Challenges to Watch

- Change management: Employees may resist or fear AI-based automation

- Data privacy: Businesses must handle data responsibly and comply with regulations

- Overdependence: AI should support, not replace, critical thinking and human oversight

- Integration: Legacy systems may not be AI-ready, requiring investment and planning

In Summary

AI is already reshaping how businesses operate across departments and industries. Whether it's improving productivity, enhancing personalization, or revealing insights from data, AI is becoming a cornerstone of modern enterprise success. As a professional, understanding how AI is applied helps you contribute to innovation, lead with insight, and prepare for the future of work.

In the next part of this book, we'll explore **Digital Marketing and Online Communication**, diving into how organizations build a digital presence through websites, email marketing, and social media—and what every professional should know to engage with it effectively.

PART 10

DIGITAL MARKETING AND ONLINE COMMUNICATION

Chapter 56
Introduction to Digital Marketing: Reaching Customers in the Digital Age

Digital marketing is the art and science of promoting products and services through digital channels. Unlike traditional marketing—billboards, flyers, and TV ads—digital marketing is measurable, targeted, and accessible to businesses of all sizes.

In today's connected world, customers are spending more time online than ever before. Whether they're searching for products, reading reviews, watching videos, or scrolling through social media, digital platforms are where decisions are made. This chapter introduces you to the core concepts of digital marketing, the key channels involved, and why every modern business needs a solid online strategy.

What Is Digital Marketing?

Digital marketing refers to any marketing activity conducted using digital technologies and channels. It spans websites, email, search engines, social media, mobile apps, and more. At its heart, digital marketing is about connecting with the right audience at the right time—and offering value in the right format.

Key Characteristics of Digital Marketing

- **Measurable**: You can track who clicked, opened, signed up, or bought

- **Targeted**: Ads and content can be shown to specific demographics, locations, or interests

- **Cost-effective**: Small businesses can start with minimal budgets

- **Interactive**: Enables two-way communication through comments, reviews, chats

- **Flexible**: Campaigns can be adjusted in real-time based on performance

Core Channels of Digital Marketing

1. **Search Engine Marketing (SEM)**

   Includes paid ads (like Google Ads) that appear when users search for specific keywords

2. **Search Engine Optimization (SEO)**

   Optimizing your website content and structure so it ranks higher in organic (non-paid) search results

3. **Social Media Marketing**

   Promoting your brand, engaging audiences, and driving traffic using platforms like Facebook, Instagram, LinkedIn, and YouTube

4. **Email Marketing**

   Sending newsletters, promotions, or updates directly to a subscriber's inbox

5. **Content Marketing**

   Creating valuable, informative, or entertaining content (blogs, videos, infographics) that attracts and retains a target audience

6. **Affiliate and Influencer Marketing**

   Partnering with individuals or websites to promote your product to their followers or readers

7. **Mobile Marketing**

   Reaching users through mobile apps, SMS campaigns, or mobile-optimized websites

Why Digital Marketing Matters

Consumers research products online before making decisions—even for offline purchases. A strong digital presence builds credibility, helps attract new customers, and keeps existing ones engaged.

Digital marketing allows businesses to:

- Compete on a level playing field with larger competitors
- Build direct relationships with their customers

- Adjust strategies quickly based on data

- Expand to new markets without opening physical locations

Real-World Example

A local bakery that once relied only on foot traffic sets up a simple website and Instagram page. With some targeted Facebook ads and regular social posts, their cake orders increase by 40% within three months. Customers now message them online, place advance orders, and leave reviews—helping grow the business far beyond walk-in traffic.

Roles and Responsibilities in Digital Marketing

Even if you're not a marketing specialist, understanding digital marketing helps you:

- Collaborate effectively with marketing teams

- Align your department's goals with customer campaigns

- Interpret website or campaign analytics

- Contribute ideas for improving online visibility and engagement

Skills and Tools to Explore

- Basic understanding of Google Analytics, Meta Ads Manager, and email campaign platforms

- Awareness of audience targeting, segmentation, and lead generation concepts

- Communication skills for writing clear and engaging copy

- Visual skills for reviewing or contributing to content creation (images, videos, banners)

In Summary

Digital marketing is essential for modern business success. Whether you're launching a new product, promoting a service, or growing a brand, reaching your audience through digital channels is no longer optional. With the right strategy, even small teams and limited budgets can achieve big results.

In the next chapter, we'll look at **Search Engine Optimization (SEO) and Website Basics**, exploring how businesses improve their visibility in search results and what it takes to build a trustworthy, effective website.

Chapter 57
Search Engine Optimization (SEO) and Website Basics: Getting Found Online

In a world where billions of searches happen on Google every day, having a website is not enough—your business needs to be discoverable. That's where **Search Engine Optimization (SEO)** comes in. SEO is the practice of optimizing your website so it ranks higher in search engine results when people look for products, services, or information related to your business.

This chapter breaks down the fundamentals of SEO and the essential elements of building a business website that not only looks professional but also performs well in search and delivers a great experience to users.

What Is SEO?

SEO stands for **Search Engine Optimization**—a set of techniques that help search engines understand and rank your website based on its relevance, quality, and usefulness. The goal is to appear among the top results when users search for topics related to your business.

There are three main types of SEO:

1. **On-Page SEO**: Optimizing the content and structure of your web pages

2. **Off-Page SEO**: Earning backlinks from other websites to build authority

3. **Technical SEO**: Improving website performance, security, and crawlability

Key SEO Elements

- **Keywords**: These are the words and phrases people type into search engines. Your content should include relevant keywords naturally, especially in titles, headers, and meta descriptions.

- **Title Tags and Meta Descriptions**: These appear in search engine results and influence whether users click on your link. They should be clear, descriptive, and include your target keywords.

- **Header Tags (H1, H2, H3)**: Organize your content and make it easier for search engines and users to understand the page structure.

- **Alt Text for Images**: Describe images using alternative text to help with accessibility and image search rankings.

- **Mobile-Friendliness**: Most users browse on mobile devices. If your site isn't responsive, it will be penalized in rankings.

- **Page Speed**: A slow-loading site leads to poor user experience and lower SEO performance. Optimize images, use caching, and minimize unnecessary scripts.

- **Internal Linking**: Linking to other relevant pages within your site helps users navigate and keeps them engaged longer.

Website Basics for Professionals

Whether you're running a business or working in one, having a basic understanding of what makes a good website is important. Here's what every professional should know:

- **Domain Name**: Choose a domain that reflects your brand and is easy to remember.

- **Hosting**: Use a reliable hosting provider with good uptime, fast speed, and security features.

- **CMS (Content Management System)**: WordPress is the most popular CMS, but there are others like Wix, Squarespace, and Webflow.

- **Design Principles**:

  - Clean and intuitive layout

  - Easy navigation

  - Clear call-to-action (e.g., Contact Us, Buy Now, Learn More)

  - Accessible and inclusive design for all users

- **Content Strategy**:

  - Focus on solving problems or answering questions your audience cares about

  - Keep content up to date and useful

  - Use a mix of formats: articles, FAQs, videos, infographics

Real-World Example

A small accounting firm wanted to increase local business. By optimizing their website with keywords like "tax consultant in Muscat" and creating blog posts answering common tax questions, they started appearing on the first page of Google. Within six months, inbound inquiries doubled without spending on ads.

Free SEO and Website Tools to Know

- **Google Search Console**: Monitor your site's performance in Google search

- **Google Analytics**: Track website visitors and user behavior

- **Yoast SEO / Rank Math (for WordPress)**: Help with on-page SEO settings

- **Ubersuggest / Ahrefs / SEMrush**: Tools for keyword research and competitor analysis

- **GTMetrix / PageSpeed Insights**: Analyze and improve page speed performance

SEO Is Not Instant

SEO is a long-term strategy. It may take weeks or months to see significant changes, especially in competitive industries. But the benefits— organic traffic, trust, and authority—make it a powerful investment for sustainable growth.

In Summary

SEO is the key to being found online without paying for ads. When paired with a well-structured, fast, and mobile-friendly website, your business becomes more visible, credible, and accessible. Whether you manage your site or collaborate with digital teams, understanding SEO and website basics helps you contribute to smarter digital strategies.

In the next chapter, we'll dive into **Social Media Marketing**, exploring how platforms like LinkedIn, Facebook, Instagram, and YouTube help businesses connect with audiences, build communities, and drive engagement.

Chapter 58
Social Media Marketing: Building Brand Presence and Engagement on LinkedIn, Facebook, Instagram, and YouTube

Social media has become a central part of how businesses connect with their audience. Whether you're promoting a product, hiring talent, educating customers, or building community, platforms like LinkedIn, Facebook, Instagram, and YouTube offer direct access to billions of users around the world.

This chapter introduces the core principles of **social media marketing**, how each major platform serves different goals, and how professionals can use social media to support branding, outreach, and business growth.

Why Social Media Marketing Matters

Social media isn't just for brand awareness—it's for interaction, feedback, storytelling, customer support, recruitment, and even direct sales. Unlike traditional marketing, social media gives businesses the chance to engage in real-time conversations and build relationships with current and potential customers.

Social media helps businesses:

- Humanize the brand and build trust

- Promote products, services, and events

- Reach specific demographics and interest groups

- Monitor public sentiment and feedback

- Drive traffic to websites or landing pages

- Generate leads and sales

Understanding Key Platforms

Each platform has a unique audience, purpose, and best practice. Knowing how to use each one strategically is essential.

LinkedIn

- A professional networking platform ideal for B2B marketing, talent acquisition, industry thought leadership, and company culture branding
- Best for: Sharing company updates, case studies, hiring announcements, professional achievements, employee highlights
- Tone: Formal, professional, insight-driven
- Audience: Decision-makers, professionals, job seekers, and industry peers

Facebook

- A versatile platform with a broad audience used for events, community building, and targeted advertising
- Best for: Engaging with local audiences, running ads, creating events, and managing customer inquiries
- Features: Pages, Groups, Messenger, Facebook Ads
- Audience: Consumers of all ages, especially 25–55+

Instagram

- A visual-first platform used to showcase products, behind-the-scenes content, company culture, and brand personality
- Best for: Photo and video content, product launches, influencer partnerships, short reels
- Features: Stories, Reels, Hashtags, Highlights, Instagram Shopping
- Audience: Younger demographic (18–35), especially useful for lifestyle, fashion, food, and creative industries

YouTube

- The world's second-largest search engine after Google, ideal for long-form video content
- Best for: Tutorials, product demos, customer testimonials, webinars, and explainer videos

- Advantages: Evergreen content, monetization opportunities, SEO value

- Audience: Wide range, including students, professionals, and decision-makers

Real-World Example

A SaaS startup uses LinkedIn to post weekly updates about new features, hiring needs, and customer success stories. On Instagram, they share office life, team events, and short videos introducing their product. They publish monthly tutorials on YouTube showing how to use their software effectively. Together, these channels create a consistent, multi-platform presence that attracts leads, partners, and talent.

Best Practices Across All Platforms

- **Consistency**: Post regularly, using a content calendar to stay organized

- **Engagement**: Respond to comments and messages promptly

- **Visuals Matter**: Use high-quality images and videos—posts with media get more views

- **Hashtags and Tags**: Use relevant hashtags to increase visibility; tag people or pages to extend reach

- **Storytelling**: Tell authentic stories instead of only posting sales content

- **Cross-Promotion**: Share content across platforms, but tailor the format and tone

- **Analytics**: Track engagement, clicks, reach, and conversions using built-in analytics tools

Content Ideas for Businesses

- Educational content: Tips, how-tos, infographics

- Behind-the-scenes: Show company culture or production process

- User-generated content: Share testimonials or customer posts

- Events and milestones: Celebrate anniversaries, new launches, awards
- Polls and questions: Invite engagement and feedback
- Live streams: Q&A sessions, webinars, product demos

Measuring Success

Social media success is not just about likes or followers. Focus on metrics that align with business goals:

- Engagement rate (likes, comments, shares per post)
- Click-through rate to your website or product pages
- Follower growth rate over time
- Conversion rate from social ads or links
- Sentiment analysis—what kind of feedback are you receiving?

Common Mistakes to Avoid

- Posting inconsistently or without a plan
- Ignoring comments or messages from followers
- Using the same content format on every platform
- Focusing only on sales and not offering value
- Overusing hashtags or using irrelevant ones
- Neglecting your profile setup—bio, logo, contact info

In Summary

Social media marketing is an essential part of building brand visibility and creating meaningful engagement with your audience. Whether you're a solo entrepreneur, a marketing professional, or part of a growing business, understanding how to leverage LinkedIn, Facebook, Instagram, and YouTube can help you connect with the right people in the right way.

In the next chapter, we'll explore **Email Marketing Tools and Strategies**, where we'll look at how email remains one of the most powerful tools for nurturing leads, building loyalty, and driving repeat business.

Chapter 59
Email Marketing Tools and Strategies: Reaching the Right People with the Right Message

Email remains one of the most effective digital marketing tools. While social media and ads often steal the spotlight, email marketing consistently delivers high returns on investment, especially for nurturing leads, engaging existing customers, and driving repeat business.

Brevo

All-in-One Platform to Manage Your Customer Relationships Via Email, SMS, Chat and More.

get.brevo.com/amjid

This chapter covers the fundamentals of email marketing, the tools used to manage campaigns, and the strategies businesses employ to ensure that their messages are not only delivered but also opened, read, and acted upon.

Why Email Marketing Still Works

- **Direct access to your audience**: You land in their inbox, not on a noisy feed.

- **Ownership**: Unlike social media, you own your email list.

- **Personalization**: You can send tailored messages based on interests, behavior, or demographics.

- **Cost-effective**: Email is cheap to scale and automation allows it to work around the clock.

- **High ROI**: Studies show email marketing often delivers $36–$45 return for every $1 spent.

Common Use Cases

- Newsletters: Regular updates to keep your audience informed

- Promotional Emails: Sales, discounts, or limited-time offers

- Drip Campaigns: Automated email sequences based on user actions

- Onboarding Series: Guide new customers or users through the product

- Event Invitations: Promote webinars, product launches, or conferences

- Re-engagement: Win back inactive subscribers or customers

Popular Email Marketing Tools

1. **Mailchimp** – User-friendly, ideal for small to medium businesses with good templates and automation.

2. **Brevo (formerly Sendinblue)** – Offers email and SMS, with strong automation and a free plan.

3. **ConvertKit** – Built for creators and content marketers, with simple tagging and automation features.

4. **HubSpot** – Ideal for enterprises needing CRM and email marketing integration.

5. **MailerLite**, **Moosend**, **Zoho Campaigns** – Other popular tools with varying strengths in ease of use, pricing, and automation.

Building a Quality Email List

A healthy email list is permission-based—meaning people chose to hear from you.

Best practices:

- Use opt-in forms on your website, blog, or checkout pages

- Offer lead magnets like eBooks, discounts, or free trials in exchange for email addresses

- Never buy email lists—this damages your domain reputation and violates privacy laws

Crafting an Effective Email Campaign

1. **Subject Line**

   o Keep it short, clear, and compelling

   o Use action verbs or curiosity to drive opens

   o Avoid ALL CAPS or spammy words like "Free!!!"

2. **Personalization**

   o Address the subscriber by name

   o Reference previous purchases, interests, or behavior

3. **Design and Layout**

   o Mobile-friendly design (more than 50% of emails are opened on mobile)

   o Clear structure with header, body, call-to-action (CTA), and footer

   o Use images sparingly and include alt text

4. **Call-to-Action (CTA)**

    ○   Tell the reader exactly what to do: "Buy Now," "Register Today," "Download Guide"

    ○   Keep it above the fold and repeated if necessary

5. **Testing and Optimization**

    ○   A/B test subject lines, send times, CTA buttons

    ○   Monitor open rates, click-through rates (CTR), and conversions

Segmentation and Automation

Instead of blasting the same message to everyone, segment your list:

- By location
- By role or job title
- By past purchases or interests
- By activity (e.g., opened last 3 emails)

Automation allows you to trigger emails based on user actions:

- Welcome emails after signup
- Reminder emails after cart abandonment
- Follow-ups after downloading a guide

Compliance and Deliverability

Stay compliant with global email laws:

- **GDPR** (Europe): Requires clear consent and unsubscribe options
- **CAN-SPAM** (US): Honest subject lines and visible contact info
- Always include an unsubscribe link
- Avoid spammy practices—over-sending, misleading links, broken formatting

Real-World Example

An online bookstore segments its email list by genre preferences. Romance readers receive curated new arrivals, while sci-fi fans get sneak peeks of upcoming releases. Automated workflows send reminders if users abandon their cart or haven't visited in 30 days. The result? Increased open rates, higher engagement, and 20% more conversions.

Key Metrics to Track

- **Open Rate** – How many recipients opened your email

- **Click-Through Rate (CTR)** – How many clicked a link inside

- **Conversion Rate** – How many took the intended action (e.g., bought a product)

- **Bounce Rate** – Emails that couldn't be delivered

- **Unsubscribe Rate** – Signals if content is irrelevant or too frequent

In Summary

Email marketing is a cornerstone of modern digital communication. With the right tools and strategies, it helps businesses build relationships, drive revenue, and keep their brand top of mind. Whether you're nurturing leads, launching products, or following up with clients, email—when done right—is a direct, powerful, and personal tool.

In the next chapter, we'll cover **Using Analytics to Optimize Campaigns**, focusing on how to track, interpret, and act on marketing data to improve performance across digital channels.

Chapter 60
Using Analytics to Optimize Campaigns: Turning Data into Marketing Decisions

Creating digital marketing campaigns is only half the job—**measuring** and **optimizing** their performance is what turns good marketing into great marketing. With powerful analytics tools now built into nearly every platform, businesses of all sizes can gain insights into what's working, what's not, and where to focus next.

This chapter explores how analytics helps marketers and business professionals make informed decisions, improve their return on investment (ROI), and continuously refine their digital marketing strategies.

Why Analytics Matter in Marketing

Without measurement, marketing is guesswork. Analytics provides:

- Clarity on customer behavior
- Proof of campaign effectiveness
- Insights for budget allocation
- Early warnings when something is underperforming
- Data to support decisions instead of relying on intuition

Whether it's a website, an email, or a social media post, tracking performance allows you to adapt quickly and improve outcomes.

Types of Marketing Analytics

1. **Website Analytics**

   Tracks user behavior on your website—who visited, how long they stayed, and what they did.

2. **Social Media Analytics**

   Shows post engagement, follower growth, reach, and audience demographics.

3. **Email Analytics**

   Includes open rates, click-through rates, conversions, and bounce rates.

4. **Advertising Analytics**

   Monitors ad performance: impressions, clicks, conversions, cost per click (CPC), and return on ad spend (ROAS).

5. **Search Analytics**

   Includes SEO data—keyword rankings, organic traffic, and click-through rates from search engines.

Popular Tools for Digital Marketing Analytics

- **Google Analytics** – Tracks website traffic, user flow, behavior, and conversions

- **Google Search Console** – Monitors your website's presence in Google search results

- **Meta Business Suite** (Facebook and Instagram) – Provides post and ad performance data

- **LinkedIn Analytics** – Offers insights into company page performance and content engagement

- **Email platforms** (like Mailchimp, Brevo) – Include dashboards for each campaign

- **UTM Parameters + Google Analytics** – Help track traffic sources for specific links

Key Metrics to Understand

- **Impressions** – How many times your content was displayed

- **Reach** – The number of unique users who saw your content

- **Click-Through Rate (CTR)** – Percentage of users who clicked a link or button

- **Conversion Rate** – Percentage of users who completed a desired action (e.g., purchase, signup)

- **Bounce Rate** – Percentage of visitors who leave your site after viewing only one page

- **Cost Per Lead (CPL)** – How much it costs to acquire a single lead

- **Return on Investment (ROI)** – Revenue generated compared to the cost of the campaign

Setting Up Campaign Tracking

Before launching a campaign:

- Define clear objectives: Are you aiming for traffic, leads, signups, or sales?

- Set KPIs (Key Performance Indicators) that align with those goals

- Use **UTM tags** to track where clicks are coming from

- Set up **goals and events** in Google Analytics to measure user actions

Using Insights to Improve Performance

Analytics isn't just about collecting data—it's about learning and acting. For example:

- If your open rates are low → improve subject lines or sender name

- If people drop off your website quickly → simplify the landing page or speed up the site

- If one ad performs better than another → shift your budget to the better-performing creative

- If visitors aren't converting → review the offer or check for technical issues

Real-World Example

A fitness coach runs a Facebook ad campaign promoting an online program. Using analytics, she notices the ad with a video gets 3x more clicks than the static image. She pauses the underperforming ads and reallocates the budget to the video version—improving ROI by 60%.

Avoiding Analysis Paralysis

While data is powerful, too much of it can become overwhelming. Focus on the **metrics that matter** to your specific goal. Not every campaign needs to track everything.

Use dashboards or summaries to make sense of trends:

- Weekly or monthly reports

- Visual charts to spot drops or spikes

- Comparisons to past campaigns or benchmarks

In Summary

Analytics turns digital marketing from an art into a science. By tracking key performance indicators and using real-time feedback, businesses can spend smarter, improve faster, and grow stronger. No matter your role in the organization, learning how to read and apply campaign data helps you make decisions that are grounded in evidence, not assumptions.

In the next chapter, we'll wrap up this section by focusing on **Digital Branding and Online Presence**—how businesses and professionals can build credibility, trust, and influence in the digital world.

Chapter 61
Digital Branding and Online Presence: Building Trust and Visibility in the Digital World

In today's competitive and connected world, your **digital brand** is often your first impression. Whether you're an individual professional, a small business, or a large organization, people search online to learn about who you are, what you offer, and whether you're credible. A strong online presence builds trust, supports marketing efforts, and helps you stay relevant in a fast-moving digital environment.

This chapter explores how to establish and manage your digital brand across platforms—your website, social media, email, search engines, and more—to create a consistent and positive experience for your audience.

What Is Digital Branding?

Digital branding is the process of creating and promoting your brand online through design, messaging, tone, content, and interactions. It's how your business or personal brand is **perceived** by people who see your digital presence.

It includes:

- Your logo and visual identity
- Website content and design
- Social media presence
- Email communication style
- Online reviews and customer feedback
- Search engine visibility and public mentions

Why Digital Presence Matters

Before contacting you, most people will:

- Google your business name

- Visit your website or social media profiles

- Read customer reviews or testimonials

- Check how active, responsive, and trustworthy you seem online

A neglected or inconsistent digital presence can cost you opportunities, while a well-managed one builds confidence and engagement.

Elements of a Strong Digital Brand

1. **Professional Website**

   ○ Clear purpose and messaging

   ○ Mobile-friendly design and fast loading

   ○ Easy navigation with updated contact info

   ○ Consistent colors, fonts, and tone

2. **Consistent Social Media Profiles**

   ○ Matching profile pictures, bios, and branding

   ○ Regular updates and engagement

   ○ Use of relevant hashtags and visuals

   ○ A tone that matches your brand personality (e.g., formal, friendly, expert, humorous)

3. **Valuable Content**

   ○ Educational blogs, videos, or infographics

   ○ Customer stories and testimonials

   ○ Behind-the-scenes insights or thought leadership posts

   ○ FAQs, guides, and helpful resources

4. **Search Visibility (SEO)**

   ○ Optimized content for keywords related to your business

   ○ Google Business Profile for local visibility

   ○ Backlinks from other trusted websites

5. **Online Reviews and Reputation**

- ○ Encouraging satisfied customers to leave reviews
- ○ Responding to feedback—positive and negative—with professionalism
- ○ Monitoring mentions of your brand online

6. **Email Presence**
- ○ Branded email signatures (logo, name, title, contact links)
- ○ Consistent and value-driven newsletters
- ○ Clear unsubscribe and privacy options

Digital Branding for Individuals (Personal Branding)

Even employees and job seekers benefit from a strong digital brand. Platforms like LinkedIn serve as digital resumes and professional portfolios.

Tips for professionals:

- Keep your LinkedIn profile updated with a clear headline and achievements
- Post or share content related to your field
- Use a professional photo and background image
- Get recommendations or endorsements from colleagues and clients

Real-World Example

A consulting firm invests in redesigning its website, aligning its color scheme and messaging across all social platforms, and training staff to use branded email signatures. Within months, they see a rise in client inquiries, improved engagement on LinkedIn, and better client retention—thanks to a more unified and trustworthy brand experience.

Brand Voice and Tone

Your digital communication should reflect your values and target audience. For example:

- A tech startup might use a casual and innovative tone
- A legal firm may stick to a formal and authoritative voice

- A personal coach might use encouraging, friendly language

Consistency in tone builds familiarity and trust.

Digital Branding Mistakes to Avoid

- Using different logos or color schemes across platforms
- Outdated website or social profiles
- Infrequent or irrelevant social media activity
- Poor grammar or unclear messaging
- Ignoring online reviews or customer feedback

In Summary

Digital branding and online presence are not just for large companies—they are essential for every modern business and professional. Your brand lives in every click, post, search result, and customer interaction. By presenting a clear, consistent, and authentic digital identity, you create lasting impressions, build credibility, and attract the opportunities that align with your goals.

In the next part of this book, we'll explore **IT Support, Career Empowerment, and Digital Growth,** guiding you through the structures behind tech support, how to build a digital-first career, and how to future-proof your skills in a rapidly changing world.

PART 11

IT SUPPORT, CAREER EMPOWERMENT, AND DIGITAL GROWTH

Chapter 62
IT Support Levels (L1, L2, L3): Understanding How Tech Support Works in Organizations

In any organization that relies on technology—and today, that means nearly every organization—IT support plays a crucial role in keeping systems running, employees productive, and disruptions minimal. But not all tech support is the same. It's structured into **levels**, each with different responsibilities, skills, and escalation paths.

This chapter explains the typical support structure—**L1, L2, and L3**—so that you understand how support tickets are handled, what to expect at each level, and how to communicate effectively with support teams to resolve issues efficiently.

Why IT Support Matters

Whether it's a password reset, a printer problem, an ERP glitch, or a system outage, users rely on IT support to get back on track quickly. A structured support model:

- Ensures faster resolution of common issues
- Prevents advanced resources from being tied up with basic tasks
- Enables escalation of complex problems to the right experts
- Keeps a record of incidents for improvement and analysis

Support Level Overview

Level 1 (L1) – Frontline Support / Help Desk

L1 is the first point of contact for users experiencing IT issues. It's typically handled by help desk staff or service desk agents who manage calls, emails, or ticketing systems.

Responsibilities

- Answering calls or responding to support tickets
- Verifying user identity and issue scope
- Basic troubleshooting: password resets, printer problems, software installation help
- Resolving frequently occurring and well-documented issues
- Creating and assigning tickets to higher levels if unresolved

Skills Required

- Good communication and customer service
- Knowledge of standard tools (Office, email, VPN, ticketing systems)
- Ability to follow scripts and use a knowledge base
- Patience and problem-solving mindset

Example

A user cannot log in to their email. The L1 agent confirms the issue, resets the password, and verifies the fix—resolving the issue in one interaction.

Level 2 (L2) – Technical and Functional Support

L2 handles more complex issues that L1 cannot resolve. These technicians have deeper knowledge of systems, applications, and technical troubleshooting.

Responsibilities

- Investigating deeper software/hardware issues
- Handling functional queries in business applications (e.g., ERP, CRM)
- Assisting with system or server access issues
- Working with logs, system diagnostics, and configuration settings
- Coordinating with vendors or third-party support as needed

Skills Required

- In-depth understanding of systems and processes

- Troubleshooting beyond user interface level

- Familiarity with databases, logs, system configuration, and application workflows

- Ability to replicate and document complex issues

Example

An ERP user sees incorrect pricing on invoices. L1 confirms it's not a UI or user error. L2 investigates item configuration, pricing rules, or synchronization issues with the database.

Level 3 (L3) – Expert and Developer-Level Support

L3 is the highest level of support, typically involving specialists, engineers, or developers. These experts handle advanced system-level issues or problems that require changes to code, infrastructure, or configurations.

Responsibilities

- Resolving bugs or issues that require code changes

- Performing system integrations or customizations

- Restoring systems after critical failures or cyberattacks

- Optimizing server performance or database configurations

- Coordinating with product vendors or architects

Skills Required

- Expert-level technical or programming knowledge

- Access to system architecture, databases, and configurations

- Root cause analysis and documentation

- Collaboration with product development or DevOps teams

Example

A custom module in the HR system is failing during payroll processing. L3 support reviews the error logs, identifies a bug in the code, and releases a patch to fix the issue permanently.

Real-World Scenario

In a logistics company:

- L1 handles forgotten passwords and printer support.

- L2 resolves delayed invoice posting in the ERP.

- L3 investigates why the mobile delivery app crashes during sync with the backend—requiring a database patch.

How Users Can Help IT Support

- Provide clear details about the issue (what you were doing, what went wrong, screenshots)

- Mention any recent changes (new software, system updates)

- Follow instructions given by support to troubleshoot

- Be respectful of the escalation process—it ensures the right resource handles the issue

The Role of Ticketing Systems

Most companies use systems like Freshdesk, ServiceNow, or Jira Service Management to:

- Log and track support tickets

- Assign priority levels (low, medium, high, urgent)

- Record resolution history

- Provide analytics for service performance

In Summary

Understanding L1, L2, and L3 IT support helps everyone in the organization know who to contact, what to expect, and how to communicate issues effectively. This structure ensures that problems are resolved quickly and efficiently, without overloading technical teams with basic queries. For both employees and managers, a little awareness goes a long way in building smoother collaboration with IT.

In the next chapter, we'll look at **Setting Up and Managing a Digital Workspace**—covering the tools, practices, and setups needed to work productively in a modern digital environment.

Chapter 63
Setting Up and Managing a Digital Workspace: Tools, Practices, and Productivity in the Modern Office

The digital workspace has become the heart of how modern professionals work—whether in the office, at home, or on the move. It includes everything from the physical setup of your desk to the virtual tools that keep you connected, collaborative, and productive.

This chapter guides you through setting up an efficient digital workspace, using essential tools, and adopting practices that help you stay focused, organized, and secure in a hybrid or fully digital work environment.

What Is a Digital Workspace?

A digital workspace is the combination of hardware, software, cloud services, and collaboration tools that allow professionals to work from anywhere. It replaces the traditional desk with a flexible, cloud-based environment where documents, apps, and communications are accessible across devices.

Why It Matters

A well-structured digital workspace:

- Boosts productivity and efficiency
- Enables remote and hybrid work
- Reduces time spent switching between tools
- Enhances collaboration
- Supports secure access to company resources

Core Components of a Digital Workspace

1. **Hardware Setup**

   ○ Reliable laptop or desktop computer with sufficient memory and storage

- Ergonomic accessories: adjustable chair, external monitor, keyboard, mouse

- Webcam and microphone for video meetings

- Docking station or USB hub for multi-device setup

- Smartphone or tablet for mobile access

2. **Connectivity and Power**

- Stable high-speed internet connection

- Backup internet (hotspot or secondary connection) for remote work

- Surge protector or UPS (Uninterruptible Power Supply) for power stability

3. **Operating System and Software**

- Updated operating system (Windows, macOS, or Linux)

- Business tools like Microsoft Office 365 or Google Workspace

- Antivirus and security software

- VPN for secure remote access

- Collaboration tools: Teams, Slack, Zoom, or Google Meet

4. **File Management and Cloud Storage**

- Cloud drives like OneDrive, Google Drive, Dropbox

- Clear folder structure for documents

- Version control and backup settings

- Shared folders for team access

5. **Task and Project Management**

- To-do list apps: Microsoft To Do, Todoist, Google Tasks

- Project boards: Trello, Asana, Monday.com, Notion

- Shared calendars with reminders and availability settings

6. **Communication Tools**
   - Email clients configured with signature and labels/folders
   - Instant messaging and channels for focused team communication
   - Scheduled status updates or check-ins with your team

Tips for Organizing a Productive Workspace

- Keep your desktop and cloud storage tidy
- Use a second monitor to extend screen space
- Set regular working hours and create daily task lists
- Mute notifications during focus periods or meetings
- Use keyboard shortcuts to save time
- Close unused tabs and apps to reduce digital clutter

Security Best Practices in the Digital Workspace

- Lock your device when not in use
- Use strong, unique passwords and enable multi-factor authentication (MFA)
- Avoid storing sensitive data on local drives
- Use approved tools only—avoid installing unauthorized software
- Regularly update all applications and operating systems
- Use secure networks or a VPN when working remotely
- Report any suspicious activity to IT immediately

Mobile Workspace Considerations

- Install official mobile apps for email, calendar, and file access
- Use mobile device management (MDM) if required by your organization
- Avoid working on public Wi-Fi without VPN protection
- Set up secure biometrics or passwords on your mobile devices

- Enable remote wipe in case of loss or theft

Real-World Example

An international sales manager uses a laptop with docking station and dual monitors at the office. On the go, they access shared files via OneDrive on their phone, attend meetings through Teams, and update client records using a mobile CRM app. With everything synced and secured, they stay productive across time zones and devices.

Digital Workspace Culture and Etiquette

- Respect others' focus time—avoid unnecessary messages or calls
- Keep virtual meetings organized with agendas and follow-ups
- Maintain your calendar to show availability
- Use shared drives and avoid emailing large attachments
- Communicate proactively about delays, deadlines, or handovers

In Summary

Setting up and managing a digital workspace isn't just an IT concern— it's essential for every professional who wants to stay efficient, secure, and connected in the modern work environment. By using the right tools, keeping your workspace organized, and following best practices, you can build a productive routine no matter where you work from.

In the next chapter, we'll explore **Career Paths in Digital, Tech, and Business**, helping you navigate the evolving landscape of professional opportunities and identify roles that match your interests and skills.

Chapter 64
Career Paths in Digital, Tech, and Business: Navigating the New Professional Landscape

The modern workplace is transforming rapidly—and so are the career opportunities within it. Today, success isn't limited to traditional roles or linear paths. From data analysts and digital marketers to IT specialists and automation consultants, new jobs are emerging at the intersection of technology, business, and innovation.

In this chapter, we'll explore various digital, tech, and business career paths, the skills required, and how professionals at all levels—from job seekers to executives—can find their place in this dynamic landscape.

The Shift in Career Thinking

Historically, career growth was seen as climbing a ladder: from junior to senior, from employee to manager. In today's digital world, career development is more like navigating a grid—with opportunities to grow **vertically**, **laterally**, or even **diagonally** as skills and industries evolve.

Companies now value:

- Adaptability and continuous learning

- Tech fluency in non-technical roles

- Problem-solving and data-informed thinking

- Collaboration across departments and geographies

Key Career Categories in the Digital Age

1. **Digital and Technology Roles**

   o **IT Support Specialist** – Solves end-user problems (L1-L3 support)

   o **Systems Administrator** – Manages servers, networks, user access, backups

   o **Network Engineer** – Designs and maintains secure communication infrastructure

   o **Cloud Engineer** – Deploys and manages cloud environments (AWS, Azure, GCP)

   o **Cybersecurity Analyst** – Protects systems and data from threats

   o **Data Analyst / Scientist** – Interprets data to support decisions

   o **AI / ML Engineer** – Builds models for automation and prediction

   o **DevOps Engineer** – Bridges development and operations for faster software delivery

2. **Business Technology and Process Roles**

   - **ERP Consultant / Business Analyst** – Improves processes using systems like SAP, Oracle, or ERPNext

   - **CRM Specialist** – Manages customer lifecycle and engagement

   - **Project Manager / Scrum Master** – Coordinates tasks, resources, and timelines

   - **Process Automation Expert** – Implements low-code tools and AI assistants

3. **Digital Marketing and Communication Roles**

   - **Digital Marketing Manager** – Plans and runs campaigns across digital channels

   - **SEO Specialist / Content Strategist** – Optimizes online visibility

   - **Email Marketing Manager** – Builds audience engagement through newsletters and sequences

   - **Social Media Manager** – Grows brand presence and community

   - **UI/UX Designer** – Enhances digital product experiences for users

4. **Hybrid Business-Technology Roles**

   - **Product Owner** – Represents business needs in software development

   - **Tech-Savvy Operations Manager** – Uses data and tools to optimize day-to-day performance

   - **Innovation / Transformation Lead** – Aligns emerging technologies with business goals

Emerging Roles Worth Exploring

- **Prompt Engineer** – Specializes in crafting inputs for AI systems

- **Automation Strategist** – Designs workflows across platforms like Zapier, Power Automate, or n8n

- **Digital Adoption Specialist** – Helps teams embrace and use new digital tools

- **Sustainability Data Analyst** – Tracks environmental impact metrics for compliance and reporting

Real-World Example

A marketing graduate joins a mid-sized firm as a content writer. Over time, she learns how to use AI tools like ChatGPT to generate content ideas, manages social media platforms, and analyzes campaign performance using Google Analytics. She upskills through certifications in SEO and email marketing and grows into the role of a digital marketing strategist—without ever writing a line of code.

How to Discover the Right Path

Ask yourself:

- What problems do I enjoy solving?

- Do I prefer working with people, systems, or ideas?

- Am I interested in building, optimizing, or managing?

- What skills come naturally to me—and which ones am I curious about?

Resources for Career Growth

- **Certifications**: PMP, ITIL, Google Analytics, Microsoft Azure, AWS, HubSpot, etc.

- **Online Courses**: Udemy, Coursera, LinkedIn Learning, edX

- **Professional Communities**: LinkedIn Groups, local tech meetups, industry associations

- **Mentorship and Networking**: Ask questions, shadow roles, or join internal learning programs

Tips for Career Transition or Advancement

- Start small: take on a tech-related project in your current role
- Document your achievements and build a portfolio (e.g., dashboards, workflows, campaigns)
- Stay current with trends in your domain
- Build a learning habit—15 minutes a day adds up quickly
- Volunteer for cross-functional teams or digital transformation initiatives

In Summary

There's never been a better time to explore a digital, tech, or hybrid business role. Whether you're just starting, looking to grow, or thinking of switching fields, the future belongs to professionals who combine curiosity, adaptability, and digital literacy. Every department now relies on tech, and every career path has a digital edge—embrace it.

In the next chapter, we'll cover **Online Identity, Branding, and Career Portfolio**, showing how to present yourself effectively online and stand out in a digital-first job market.

Chapter 65
Online Identity, Branding, and Career Portfolio: Standing Out in the Digital-First Job Market

In a world where hiring managers, clients, and collaborators often search your name before they meet you, your **online identity** becomes your first impression. Whether you're applying for a job, networking with peers, or building authority in your field, having a strong personal brand and a well-crafted career portfolio can set you apart.

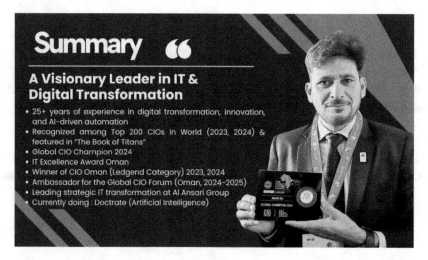

This chapter explores how to shape your online identity, build a compelling digital presence, and showcase your skills and experience through a professional portfolio that reflects who you are and what you bring to the table.

What Is Online Identity and Personal Branding?

Your **online identity** is the sum of your digital presence—LinkedIn profile, personal website, online comments, blog posts, videos, public forums, and more. Your **personal brand** is how people perceive you professionally based on what they see, read, and hear.

In short:

- Your identity is your visibility.

- Your brand is your value.

Why It Matters

- Hiring managers check LinkedIn and social media before interviews

- Clients assess credibility through Google searches and testimonials

- Partners and peers seek signals of thought leadership, skills, and attitude

- Opportunities (freelance, collaborations, speaking engagements) often come from being visible and trusted online

Key Elements of a Strong Online Presence

1. **Professional LinkedIn Profile**

   o Clear, keyword-rich headline (not just your job title)

   o Updated work history with measurable accomplishments

   o Custom LinkedIn URL

   o Profile photo and banner that reflect your industry

   o Summary that tells your story—not just a list of skills

2. **Career Portfolio or Personal Website**

   o Includes a bio, resume, project samples, testimonials, certifications

   o Acts as a central place to showcase your work

   o Tools: WordPress, Wix, Carrd, Notion, GitHub (for tech portfolios)

3. **Professional Email and Signature**

   o Use a professional email (ideally with your name or domain)

   o Add a signature with name, title, LinkedIn link, and contact info

4. **Content and Thought Leadership**

   o Share relevant content (articles, insights, opinions) in your domain

   o Write LinkedIn posts or blog articles that reflect your expertise

   o Comment thoughtfully on others' content—engagement builds visibility

5. **Consistent Visual Identity**

   o Use the same headshot, colors, and bio across platforms

   o Avoid conflicting or outdated information on different sites

Building a Digital Career Portfolio

Whether you're in marketing, tech, operations, or leadership, a digital portfolio helps you prove your skills with evidence.

Include:

- Project case studies: What was the challenge, your role, and the outcome?

- Visuals: Screenshots of dashboards, presentations, campaigns, workflows

- Metrics: Results achieved—% improvement, savings, growth

- Certifications and continuing education

- Testimonials from supervisors, peers, or clients

- Optional: Video intro or project walkthrough

Real-World Example

A mid-career IT project manager creates a simple Notion site showcasing successful ERP implementations, certifications (PMP, ITIL), and client feedback. They link it on LinkedIn and in their email signature. During interviews, they walk through the site to explain their experience—leaving a memorable impression and reinforcing their credibility.

Best Practices for Managing Your Digital Identity

- Google your name occasionally—see what others see

- Update your profiles at least once every six months

- Separate personal and professional social media (or manage privacy settings carefully)

- Avoid posting controversial, aggressive, or polarizing content if it's tied to your professional identity

- Use your real name or a consistent handle across platforms

Common Mistakes to Avoid

- Incomplete or outdated profiles

- Using generic summaries that don't reflect your actual value

- Having a cluttered or unprofessional personal website

- Ignoring typos, poor formatting, or broken links

- Being silent online—no presence is often seen as no activity

In Summary

Your online identity is your modern business card. It's active, searchable, and influential. By investing time in your digital brand and portfolio, you don't just tell people who you are—you show them. In a digital-first world, this visibility and credibility are key to unlocking professional growth, building trust, and standing out in a crowded marketplace.

In the next chapter, we'll focus on **Lifelong Learning and Staying Technologically Relevant**, a mindset and strategy that helps you future-proof your career in the ever-evolving world of work.

Chapter 66
Lifelong Learning and Staying Technologically Relevant: Future-Proofing Your Career

Technology is changing faster than ever. New tools, platforms, and roles are constantly emerging—reshaping industries, job requirements, and the way we work. In this environment, the most valuable skill is the ability to learn continuously. Whether you're just entering the workforce or have decades of experience, **lifelong learning** is the key to staying relevant, adaptable, and empowered in the digital age.

This chapter explores why continuous learning matters, how to build a habit of learning, and what strategies and resources you can use to stay current in your field—no matter what your role is.

Why Lifelong Learning Matters

- **Skills have a shorter shelf life**: Tools and practices that were cutting-edge five years ago may now be obsolete.

- **Jobs are evolving**: Roles like AI Prompt Engineer, Automation Strategist, or Remote IT Support Lead didn't exist a decade ago.

- **Organizations expect growth**: Employers want people who take initiative, solve problems, and stay ahead of change.

- **Learning builds confidence**: You don't have to fear change when you know how to adapt to it.

Real-World Examples

- An HR professional who upskills in HR analytics can move into a data-driven strategic role.

- A finance manager who learns Power BI or Excel automation becomes more efficient and insightful in reporting.

- A small business owner who understands digital marketing can reduce costs and improve online visibility.

What Does Lifelong Learning Look Like in Practice?

1. **Microlearning**
   - Short, focused lessons or articles that fit into your daily schedule
   - Examples: watching a 10-minute tutorial, reading an industry blog, or completing a LinkedIn Learning video

2. **Certifications and Courses**
   - Structured programs to build or validate new skills
   - Platforms: Udemy, Coursera, LinkedIn Learning, edX, Skillshare
   - Topics: IT, cloud, cybersecurity, data analytics, digital marketing, project management, etc.

3. **Reading and Research**
   - Follow thought leaders, newsletters, white papers, blogs, and podcasts in your domain
   - Examples: Harvard Business Review, Medium, TechCrunch, Wired, Gartner

4. **Peer Learning**
   - Join internal learning circles or external communities
   - Participate in webinars, panels, or knowledge-sharing sessions
   - Ask colleagues about the tools they're using and what they've learned recently

5. **Hands-On Projects**
   - Apply what you learn in real or simulated projects
   - Build dashboards, automate a process, write a blog post, or contribute to open-source projects

6. **Certifications That Stay Relevant**
   - Technology: Microsoft, AWS, Cisco, Google Cloud, CompTIA
   - Management: PMP, Agile, Scrum, ITIL

○ Business and Analytics: Power BI, Tableau, Six Sigma, HubSpot

Creating a Personal Learning Plan

You don't need to learn everything. Focus on what supports your current role—or the role you want next.

Steps to create your plan:

1. Identify your career goals (short and long term)

2. Assess current skill gaps

3. Set a realistic learning schedule (e.g., 3 hours a week)

4. Choose formats that fit your style (video, reading, mentoring, hands-on)

5. Track your progress and update your resume or portfolio as you grow

Mindset Shift: From Formal Learning to Everyday Learning

Learning doesn't only happen in classrooms. You can learn by:

• Watching a YouTube tutorial during lunch

• Reading industry updates on your commute

• Shadowing a colleague using a tool you haven't mastered yet

• Asking better questions in meetings or support groups

Tools and Platforms to Explore

• **Udemy**: Affordable, practical courses on business and tech

• **Coursera**: University-level programs with certificates

• **LinkedIn Learning**: Business, software, and personal development skills

• **n8n Academy, Microsoft Learn, AWS Skill Builder, Google Digital Garage**

- **Notion / Obsidian**: Tools to organize and review what you're learning

Avoiding Burnout While Learning

- Don't try to master everything at once

- Take breaks and reflect on what you've learned

- Choose what's relevant to your interests and goals

- Mix learning with application—try out new tools or teach someone else

In Summary

Lifelong learning is not optional in the digital age—it's your most powerful career strategy. The more you learn, the more opportunities you create for yourself. Whether you're growing within your current role, preparing for a future shift, or building your own business, staying technologically relevant ensures you stay in control of your journey.

With curiosity, commitment, and a few smart strategies, you can future-proof your career and lead confidently in a world that never stops changing.

Appendices

This section provides supporting materials, tools, and resources that reinforce key concepts covered in the book. It serves as a practical reference for readers to continue learning, apply knowledge, and implement digital best practices in their work and life.

Appendix A: Glossary of Terms

This glossary provides simple, business-friendly definitions of common terms used throughout the book. It is designed to serve as a quick reference for readers who want to better understand digital terminology in context.

AI (Artificial Intelligence): Technology that enables machines or software to mimic human intelligence—such as learning, decision-making, language understanding, and visual recognition.

API (Application Programming Interface) : A set of rules and protocols that allow different software systems to communicate with each other.

Automation: The use of technology to perform tasks with minimal human intervention, often used in workflows, manufacturing, and administrative processes.

Backup: A copy of important data stored in a secure location, used to recover information in case of loss, damage, or cyberattack.

BI (Business Intelligence): Tools and systems that collect, analyze, and present business data to help decision-makers gain insights and make informed choices.

Browser: Software used to access websites and online applications. Examples include Chrome, Firefox, Edge, and Safari.

Cloud Computing: Using internet-based servers to store, manage, and process data instead of local computers or on-premises servers.

CRM (Customer Relationship Management): Software systems that help businesses manage interactions with customers and track sales, support, and communication.

Cybersecurity: The practice of protecting systems, networks, and data from unauthorized access, attacks, or damage.

Data Governance: The framework for managing data availability, usability, integrity, and security in an organization.

Digital Workspace: A virtual environment that allows users to access files, tools, and communication systems from anywhere using the internet.

Email Signature: A block of text added automatically at the end of an email, usually containing the sender's name, title, contact info, and company branding.

Encryption: The process of converting information into a secure format that can only be read by someone with the correct key or password.

ERP (Enterprise Resource Planning): A system that integrates core business processes—like finance, HR, sales, inventory—into a single platform.

Firewall: A security system that controls incoming and outgoing network traffic to protect against unauthorized access.

IaaS / PaaS / SaaS (Cloud Models)

- IaaS: Infrastructure as a Service (e.g., virtual servers)
- PaaS: Platform as a Service (e.g., development tools)
- SaaS: Software as a Service (e.g., email, CRM, ERP apps)

Incident Reporting: The process of documenting and communicating any security or operational issue that affects systems or data.

IT Support Levels (L1, L2, L3)

- L1: Basic technical support and issue logging
- L2: More complex problem-solving by technical staff
- L3: Expert-level support and troubleshooting requiring code or infrastructure changes

KPI (Key Performance Indicator): A measurable value that helps evaluate how effectively a person, team, or system is achieving its goals.

Malware: Malicious software, such as viruses, worms, or ransomware, designed to harm or exploit computer systems.

MFA (Multi-Factor Authentication): A security measure that requires users to verify their identity using more than one method—such as a password and a mobile code.

Phishing: A cyberattack technique where fake emails or messages trick users into revealing sensitive information or downloading malware.

Prompt Engineering: The art of crafting effective instructions or queries for AI systems like ChatGPT to get relevant, high-quality outputs.

Remote Work Security: Practices and tools used to keep data and devices secure when employees work from home or outside the office network.

Social Engineering: Manipulative tactics used by attackers to trick people into giving away confidential information or performing unsafe actions.

Two-Factor Authentication (2FA): A form of multi-factor authentication where two types of verification are required to access an account or system.

User Access Control: A method of managing who can access specific systems, applications, or files based on their role or need.

Virtual Machine (VM): A software-based computer that runs within another computer, allowing multiple systems to operate on the same physical hardware.

VPN (Virtual Private Network): A secure connection that encrypts your internet traffic, often used to safely access company resources from remote locations.

Workflow Automation: Using software to automate repetitive business tasks such as approvals, notifications, and data transfers between systems.

Appendix B: Security and Productivity Checklists

These checklists are designed to help individuals and teams adopt essential digital habits. Use them to improve personal efficiency, secure your devices, and maintain a professional digital work environment—whether you're working from an office or remotely.

Daily Cybersecurity Checklist (for Employees)

- Lock your device when stepping away
- Avoid clicking links in suspicious emails or messages
- Verify the sender's email address before responding to requests
- Log out of systems you're not using
- Use secure Wi-Fi or VPN when working remotely
- Do not plug in unknown USB devices
- Avoid saving passwords in browsers without encryption

Weekly Digital Hygiene Checklist

- Restart your computer to apply pending updates
- Check for software or browser updates
- Clear temporary files and browser cache
- Review your downloads folder and delete unnecessary files
- Run a full antivirus/malware scan
- Verify that all files are syncing correctly to your cloud storage
- Back up important files if not done automatically

Remote Work Security Checklist

- Use multi-factor authentication (MFA) for all work apps
- Ensure VPN is active when accessing company systems
- Work in a private space where confidential information can't be seen or overheard
- Turn off smart speakers or digital assistants during work meetings

- Avoid using personal email or cloud storage for work files
- Use a company-approved mobile device management (MDM) tool if required
- Disconnect from work apps when not working (especially on shared devices)

Digital Productivity Checklist

- Organize files into properly named folders
- Use a to-do list or task manager to plan your day
- Block calendar time for deep work and avoid multitasking
- Use keyboard shortcuts to speed up document editing
- Respond to priority emails in the first hour of your day
- Archive or delete unnecessary emails at the end of each day
- End each day by reviewing tasks completed and preparing for the next

Monthly Workplace IT Check (Managers or Team Leads)

- Confirm backups are running and tested
- Review access rights for team members (remove unnecessary permissions)
- Review incident logs or tickets for recurring problems
- Schedule a cybersecurity awareness tip or short training
- Evaluate software or app usage—remove or consolidate unused tools
- Test business continuity and remote access procedures

Device Health Checklist

- Battery health: Check for swelling or charging issues
- Disk space: Keep at least 20% of storage free
- System performance: Monitor for lag or overheating
- Clean hardware: Keyboard, screen, and ventilation
- Label your device with contact info (for loss recovery)

Appendix C: Bash and Command Line Reference

The command line is a powerful interface for interacting with your system. It allows for greater control over your computer, enabling quick execution of tasks, automation, and troubleshooting. This reference guide covers the most commonly used Bash commands for file management, system operations, and networking.

Basic File Operations

- Ls

  Lists files and directories in the current directory.

  ls -l (lists files with detailed information), ls -a (lists all files including hidden)

- Cd

  Changes the current directory.

  cd /path/to/directory (navigate to a specific directory)

  cd .. (move one level up)

- Pwd

  Prints the working directory (shows your current directory).

- Cp

  Copies files or directories.

  cp source.txt destination.txt

- Mv

  Moves or renames files.

  mv oldname.txt newname.txt

- Rm

  Removes files or directories.

  rm file.txt (remove a file)

  rm -r folder/ (remove a directory recursively)

- Touch

Creates an empty file or updates the timestamp of an existing file.

touch newfile.txt

Permissions and Ownership

- **Chmod**

  Changes the permissions of a file or directory.

  chmod 755 file.txt (read, write, execute for owner; read and execute for others)

- **Chown**

  Changes the ownership of a file or directory.

  chown user:group file.txt

- **Chgrp**

  Changes the group ownership of a file.

  chgrp group file.txt

System Monitoring

- **top**

  Displays a real-time list of system processes and their resource usage (CPU, memory).

  top

- **htop**

  An enhanced version of top with a more user-friendly interface (may need to be installed).

- **Df**

  Shows disk space usage of all mounted filesystems.

  df -h (human-readable format)

- **Du**

  Shows disk usage of files and directories.

  du -sh * (disk usage of files in current directory)

- **Free**

  Displays memory usage.

  free -h (human-readable format)

- **Uptime**

  Displays how long the system has been running, load averages, and the number of logged-in users.
  uptime

Network Commands

- **Ping**

  Tests the connection to another host (e.g., checking network connectivity to a server).

  ping 8.8.8.8

- **Ifconfig**

  Displays or configures network interface parameters.

  ifconfig -a (show all interfaces)

- **Netstat**

  Shows active network connections and listening ports.

  netstat -tuln (show TCP and UDP listening ports)

- **Curl**

  Transfers data from or to a server using various protocols (e.g., HTTP, FTP).

  curl http://example.com

- **Wget**

  Retrieves files from the web (useful for downloading files).

  wget http://example.com/file.tx

Process Management

- **Ps**

  Displays a snapshot of current processes.

309

ps aux (show all running processes)

- **Kill**

  Terminates processes.

  kill PID (terminate a process by its Process ID)

- **Killall**

  Terminates processes by name.

  killall processname

- **Bg**

  Resumes a paused job in the background.

  bg %1 (resume job number 1 in the background)

- **Fg**

  Brings a background job to the foreground.

  fg %1 (bring job number 1 to the foreground)

Text Processing

- **Cat**

  Concatenates and displays file content.

  cat file.txt (display file content)

- **Grep**

  Searches for patterns in files.

  grep "search_term" filename.txt

- **Find**

  Searches for files and directories in a specified location.

  find /path/to/search -name "*.txt" (find all .txt files)

- **Sed**

  Stream editor for modifying text in files.

  sed 's/old/new/g' file.txt (replace "old" with "new" globally in the file)

- Awk

  Pattern scanning and processing language, commonly used for data manipulation.

  awk '{print $1}' file.txt (prints the first column of a file

Package Management

- apt-get (Debian-based systems)

  Installs, updates, and removes software packages.

  sudo apt-get install package_name (install a package)

  sudo apt-get update (update package lists)

- yum (Red Hat-based systems)

  Manages packages and updates.

  sudo yum install package_name (install a package

- pacman (Arch Linux)

  Package manager for Arch-based distributions.

  sudo pacman -S package_name (install a package)

Archiving and Compression

- tar

  Creates compressed archives.

  tar -czvf archive.tar.gz directory/ (create a .tar.gz archive)

- zip / unzip

  Compress and extract .zip archives.

  zip archive.zip files/ (create a .zip file)

  unzip archive.zip (extract a .zip file)

- gzip / gunzip

  Compress and extract .gz files.

  gzip file.txt (compress file)

  gunzip file.txt.gz (decompress file)

System Administration and Maintenance

- **sudo**

    Runs commands with superuser (root) privileges.

    sudo apt-get update (update package list with admin privileges)

- **shutdown**

    Powers off or restarts the system.

    sudo shutdown -h now (shutdown immediately)

    sudo shutdown -r now (restart immediately)

- **reboot**

    Restarts the system.

    sudo reboot

Appendix D: Guide for Poster Templates and Awareness Materials

This section provides templates and suggested content for creating visual awareness materials that can be used in the workplace or distributed digitally. These posters are intended to promote security best practices, improve productivity, and raise awareness of digital habits among employees.

1. Password Security Poster

Title: "Your First Line of Defense: Strong Passwords"

- **Key Points:**
  - Use a unique password for every account.
  - Ensure passwords are at least 12 characters long.
  - Include a mix of letters (upper and lower case), numbers, and special characters.
  - Avoid using personal information like birthdays or names.
  - Enable multi-factor authentication (MFA) wherever possible.
  - Change your passwords regularly, especially for critical accounts.

- **Visuals:**
  - Image of a lock with a digital fingerprint.
  - A simple chart comparing weak versus strong passwords (e.g., "password123" vs. "G$9!B@w2kP1").

2. Phishing Awareness Poster

Title: "Don't Get Hooked! Recognizing Phishing Emails"

- **Key Points:**
  - **Look for suspicious signs**: Unusual sender address, urgent tone, and unsolicited attachments or links.

- o **Check the email address**: Phishers often use slight variations of legitimate addresses (e.g., @microsft.com vs. @microsoft.com).
- o **Don't click links or open attachments**: Hover over links to see the destination URL. If you're unsure, type the website's address manually.
- o **Verify**: Call or email the person or company directly using known contact details to verify requests.
- o **Report**: If you receive a suspicious email, report it to your IT department.
- **Visuals:**
  - o Image of a fish with a hook labeled "Phishing."
  - o Sample phishing email showing tell-tale signs (e.g., mismatched URL, unsolicited request for sensitive info).

3. Safe Browsing Poster

Title: "Browse Safely and Smartly!"

- **Key Points:**
  - o Always ensure the website has "HTTPS://" and a padlock symbol before entering sensitive information.
  - o Don't visit untrusted websites or click on pop-up ads.
  - o Avoid downloading files from unknown sources.
  - o Use strong security software to protect against malicious sites.
  - o Regularly update your browser to ensure it is equipped with the latest security patches.
- **Visuals:**
  - o Screenshot of a browser URL bar showing "https://" and a padlock.
  - o Illustration of a browser with a "danger zone" warning for unsafe sites.

4. Mobile Device Security Poster

Title: "Keep Your Mobile Secure and Protected!"

- **Key Points:**

  - **Set a strong password**: Use a PIN, pattern, or biometric authentication like fingerprint or face recognition.

  - **Enable remote wipe**: Ensure your device can be wiped remotely if it's lost or stolen.

  - **Install apps from trusted sources**: Only download apps from official app stores like Google Play or Apple's App Store.

  - **Use a VPN**: Always use a VPN to secure your connection when accessing work-related apps or websites on public Wi-Fi.

  - **Update regularly**: Keep your phone's operating system and apps up to date.

- **Visuals:**

  - Image of a mobile phone with a lock and biometric fingerprint.

  - A checklist highlighting mobile security steps.

5. Safe Internet Use Poster

Title: "Surf Safely, Protect Yourself Online!"

- **Key Points:**

  - Use strong, unique passwords for every site you visit.

  - Enable two-factor authentication (2FA) for additional security.

  - Be cautious about what personal information you share online.

  - Watch out for social engineering attacks—don't trust everyone you meet online.

  - If in doubt, don't click. Always verify before taking action.

- **Visuals:**

  ○ Illustration of a shield protecting a laptop, symbolizing internet safety.

  ○ A warning symbol next to a suspicious-looking link.

6. Work From Home Best Practices Poster

Title: "Working from Home? Stay Productive and Secure!"

- **Key Points:**

  ○ **Secure your network**: Use a VPN when working from home to secure your internet connection.

  ○ **Keep devices locked**: Lock your computer and phone when not in use.

  ○ **Be mindful of the environment**: Avoid working in public spaces where others might see confidential information.

  ○ **Use company-approved tools**: Stick to approved platforms for communication and file sharing to avoid security risks.

  ○ **Stay organized**: Create a dedicated workspace for maximum productivity and minimal distractions.

- **Visuals:**

  ○ A home office illustration with a computer, secure Wi-Fi icon, and lock symbol.

  ○ A list of "Do's and Don'ts" for remote workers.

7. Email Communication Etiquette Poster

Title: "Mastering Professional Email Etiquette"

- **Key Points:**

  ○ Always use a clear subject line and a professional tone.

  ○ Be concise: Keep emails short and to the point.

  ○ Use a proper greeting and closing.

  ○ Be mindful of the "Reply All" function—only use it when necessary.

316

- ○ Avoid informal language or slang in professional emails.
- **Visuals:**
  - ○ A well-organized email inbox with a "Reply All" warning.
  - ○ Icons representing email components (subject, greeting, body, signature).

8. Data Backup and Recovery Poster

Title: "Don't Lose Your Work! Backup Your Data Regularly"

- **Key Points:**
  - ○ **Backup regularly**: Ensure your files are automatically backed up to the cloud or external storage.
  - ○ **Follow the 3-2-1 Rule**: 3 copies of your data, 2 types of media, and 1 off-site.
  - ○ **Test your backups**: Regularly verify that your backup files can be restored.
  - ○ **Use encryption**: Ensure backup files are encrypted to protect sensitive data.
- **Visuals:**
  - ○ Illustration of a cloud backup service with arrows pointing to a hard drive and remote server.
  - ○ A checklist of backup procedures with tick marks.

How to Use These Materials

You can use Canva to create posters and then these posters can be printed and displayed in office spaces, break rooms, or meeting areas to reinforce good practices. Alternatively, they can be shared digitally via email, internal portals, or social media platforms to keep employees engaged and aware of the latest best practices.

Appendix E: Tool Recommendations and Learning Platforms

In the ever-evolving digital landscape, the right tools and platforms can significantly boost your productivity, learning, and security. The list of recommended tools in this section serves as a guide to help you navigate the most effective software and services available today.

Explore the Latest Tools on SyncBricks

Please note that tools and platforms are constantly evolving, and new ones frequently emerge. To stay up-to-date with the most current recommendations, explore syncbricks.com and amjidali.com where you can find an updated list of the best tools and resources across various categories—whether it's for productivity, cybersecurity, project management, or learning.

For up to date courses visit **lms.syncbricks.com**,

1. Productivity and Collaboration Tools

Microsoft 365 / Google Workspace

- **Purpose**: Office suite for document creation, collaboration, and cloud storage.

- **Best for**: Document editing, presentations, spreadsheets, and email.

- **Key Features**: Real-time collaboration, cloud storage, scheduling, and task management.

Trello / Asana / Monday.com

- **Purpose**: Project and task management tools for teams and individuals.

- **Best for**: Task tracking, project planning, team collaboration.

- **Key Features**: Kanban boards, task assignments, deadlines, and integrations with other tools.

Slack / Microsoft Teams

- **Purpose**: Messaging and collaboration platforms for team communication.
- **Best for**: Remote teams, internal communication, and project-specific channels.
- **Key Features**: Instant messaging, file sharing, video calls, and integrations.

Zoom / Google Meet

- **Purpose**: Video conferencing and virtual meeting platforms.
- **Best for**: Virtual meetings, webinars, team collaboration.
- **Key Features**: Screen sharing, breakout rooms, meeting scheduling.

2. Security and Privacy Tools

Bitwarden / 1Password / LastPass

- **Purpose**: Password management and secure login storage.
- **Best for**: Storing and organizing passwords securely.
- **Key Features**: Encrypted password storage, auto-fill, multi-device syncing.

ProtonMail / Tutanota

- **Purpose**: Encrypted email services for privacy-conscious users.
- **Best for**: Secure, privacy-first email communication.
- **Key Features**: End-to-end encryption, anonymous email services.

NordVPN / ExpressVPN

- **Purpose**: VPN services for secure internet connections.
- **Best for**: Protecting your data and ensuring privacy while browsing.
- **Key Features**: Anonymous browsing, encrypted connections, geo-location masking.

Malwarebytes / Bitdefender

- **Purpose**: Antivirus and anti-malware software for endpoint protection.

- **Best for**: Preventing and removing malicious software from your devices.

- **Key Features**: Real-time protection, malware removal, system scans.

3. Workflow Automation Tools

Zapier / Make.com (formerly Integromat)

- **Purpose**: Automates workflows by connecting different apps and services.

- **Best for**: Integrating and automating tasks across apps like Gmail, Slack, and Trello.

- **Key Features**: No-code automation, app integrations, multi-step workflows.

n8n.syncbricks.com

- **Purpose**: Open-source workflow automation tool for developers and non-developers alike.

- **Best for**: Automating workflows between apps, APIs, and cloud services.

- **Key Features**: Workflow builder, custom integrations, self-hosting option.

Microsoft Power Automate

- **Purpose**: Automates repetitive tasks and workflows using Microsoft apps.

- **Best for**: Integration within Microsoft 365 ecosystem.

- **Key Features**: Pre-built templates, business process automation, approval workflows.

4. Business Intelligence and Data Visualization Tools

Power BI

- **Purpose**: Data visualization and business intelligence tool by Microsoft.

- **Best for**: Creating reports and dashboards from various data sources.

- **Key Features**: Data modeling, interactive visualizations, reporting.

Tableau

- **Purpose**: A powerful data visualization tool.

- **Best for**: Analyzing large data sets and sharing visual reports.

- **Key Features**: Drag-and-drop interface, data blending, analytics.

Google Data Studio

- **Purpose**: Free, web-based data visualization tool.

- **Best for**: Connecting various data sources and creating interactive reports.

- **Key Features**: Customizable reports, Google Analytics integration, collaboration.

5. Learning Platforms

Udemy

- **Purpose**: Online learning platform offering thousands of courses on a variety of topics.

- **Best for**: Skill-building, certifications, and professional development.

- **Key Features**: Video tutorials, downloadable resources, lifetime access to courses.

Coursera

- **Purpose**: Provides online courses from top universities and organizations.

- **Best for**: Advanced certifications, university-level courses, professional credentials.

- **Key Features**: Peer-reviewed assignments, professional certificates, specializations.

LinkedIn Learning

- **Purpose**: Professional development platform with courses on business, tech, and creative skills.

- **Best for**: Learning practical skills and soft skills.

- **Key Features**: Integration with LinkedIn profile, personalized course recommendations, certificates of completion.

edX

- **Purpose**: Offers online courses from universities and institutions around the world.

- **Best for**: MOOCs (Massive Open Online Courses) in fields like IT, business, data science.

- **Key Features**: Self-paced learning, certificates, degree programs.

Skillshare

- **Purpose**: Creative-focused online learning platform with courses on design, art, business, and more.

- **Best for**: Creative professionals and entrepreneurs.

- **Key Features**: Project-based learning, community feedback, free trials.

6. Open-Source Tools

ERPNext

- **Purpose**: Open-source ERP system for businesses of all sizes.

- **Best for**: Small-to-medium enterprises looking for an affordable, customizable ERP solution.

- **Key Features**: Accounting, HR, sales, inventory, and project management modules.

Odoo

- **Purpose**: Open-source ERP solution with an integrated suite of apps.

- **Best for**: Businesses that need customizable software for management.

- **Key Features**: CRM, project management, sales, website builder, and more.

GitHub

- **Purpose**: Code hosting and version control platform for software developers.

- **Best for**: Storing code, collaborating on open-source projects, version tracking.

- **Key Features**: Code repository, pull requests, issue tracking.

Appendix F: Self-Assessment Quizzes

While self-assessment quizzes can be an invaluable tool for reinforcing your understanding of the material, the interactive nature of quizzes is better suited to an online format. To help you test your knowledge and track your progress, I've made available a series of quizzes based on the content of this book. These quizzes are hosted on my LMS at lms.syncbricks.com.

How to Access the Quizzes:

- Scan the **QR code** below to access the quizzes on your mobile device.

- Visit lms.syncbricks.com/quiz/it to find up-to-date quizzes and assessments across all book chapters.

Appendix G: Companion Course and Video Resources

To support your learning journey and deepen your understanding of the concepts covered in **"Mastering Information Technology: A Practical Guide for Beginners, Professionals & Business Leaders"**, I have created a comprehensive online companion course titled:

"Essential Tech Skills for Today's Professionals: A Step-by-Step Learning Journey"

This course is designed to complement the book by offering practical lessons, video tutorials, and quizzes that you can use to solidify your knowledge and apply it to real-world scenarios.

What You'll Get:

- **In-depth video lessons** that expand on key concepts from each chapter.

- **Practical examples** and real-world applications to help you see how these skills translate into the workplace.

- **Interactive quizzes** that reinforce your learning and provide instant feedback.

- **Downloadable resources**, such as templates and checklists to support your digital journey.

The course will be continually updated with new content to ensure it remains relevant to the ever-evolving world of technology.

How to Access the Course:

- Scan the **QR code** below to access the companion course directly from your mobile device.

- Visit **lms.syncbricks.com** for the full course catalog and updates.

Conclusion
Empowering the Future of Work

As we reach the end of this journey through the vast world of information technology, it's important to remember that mastering these skills is not just about understanding tools, systems, or concepts. It's about **empowering yourself to thrive in the digital world**—whether you're just starting your career, advancing in your current role, or leading a team or business.

The landscape of modern work is dynamic and constantly evolving, and by mastering the core principles of computing, networking, cybersecurity, business applications, and digital productivity, you've equipped yourself with a foundation that will serve you throughout your career. Whether you are using IT to solve problems, enhance productivity, or drive innovation, these skills will open doors to new opportunities and keep you ahead of the curve.

Key Takeaways:

- Embrace **lifelong learning**. The tech world evolves quickly, and staying relevant means adapting to new tools, techniques, and best practices.

- Focus on **practical application**. It's not just about theory; it's about using your skills to solve real-world problems and create value for yourself, your team, or your business.

- Build a **digital presence** that reflects your expertise. Showcase your skills, certifications, and projects online, and use your personal brand to stand out in the professional world.

- **Stay curious and adaptable**. The future of work will be shaped by new technologies, and the professionals who thrive will be those who embrace change and continue to learn.

As you continue your journey, remember that technology is a tool, not an end goal. It's how you use it that matters. Whether you're optimizing a business process, enhancing team collaboration, securing data, or driving digital transformation, **your ability to harness the power of technology will shape the future of your career and the world around you**.

Thank you for taking this step toward mastering information technology. Now, go forth with confidence, and continue to build, innovate, and lead in a world that is increasingly driven by digital progress.

About the Author

Amjid Ali is an accomplished **CIO, Digital Visionary**, and **Educator** with over 25 years of experience in the Information Technology field. Throughout his career, he has helped businesses across various industries leverage technology to drive digital transformation, improve business processes, and enhance productivity.

Amjid's expertise spans a wide array of areas, including cloud migration, ERP systems, cybersecurity, AI integration, automation, business intelligence, and IT infrastructure. As a consultant and thought leader, he works with businesses, organizations, and professionals to help them adapt to the rapidly changing digital landscape.

He is also the author of several educational resources and online courses, helping individuals enhance their technical knowledge and bridge the gap between business and IT.

In addition to his professional experience, Amjid is passionate about educating the next generation of digital leaders and empowering individuals to thrive in an increasingly tech-driven world. Through his platform, **lms.syncbricks.com**, and his website **amjidali.com**, he provides valuable resources, tools, and personalized consulting to guide individuals and organizations in their digital transformation journeys.

Scan the QR Code to follow him on LinkedIn

For more information, you can visit his website at amjidali.com or contact him directly at **amjid@amjidali.com**.

www.ingramcontent.com/pod-product-compliance
Lightning Source LLC
LaVergne TN
LVHW051430050326
832903LV00030BD/3000